Cadillac

100 Years

of Innovation

©2003 Krause Publications

Published by

krause publications
An F&W Publications Company

700 East State Street • Iola, WI 54990-0001
715-445-2214 • 888-457-2873
www.krause.com

Our toll-free number to place an order or obtain a
free catalog is 800-258-0929.

Library of Congress Catalog Number: 2003108882

ISBN: 0-87349-690-6

Edited by Brian Earnest

Designed by Gary Carle

Printed in the United States of America

Dedication

For my parents, Michael and Debbie Van Bogart, who first accepted,
and then adopted, my Cadillac obsession.

Acknowledgments

Opening a good book should be like firing the engine of your Cadillac, easing the chrome gear selector into "drive," and going for a jaunt down an unfamiliar, tree-lined back road on a cool fall day. With the rainbow of leaves masking the bends and corners of the black trail ahead, a feeling of excitement may pound in your heart as your Cadillac moves you swiftly and confidently through the turns until you arrive at an unknown destination that was begging for a visit.

In leafing through this book, I hope that same thrill of a drive behind the wheel of your own Cadillac or the dream of a drive in the crested machine of your fantasies overtakes your senses. With the help of General Motors Media Archives and many fellow Cadillac LaSalle Club, International members, I have tried to make the trip as scenic as possible while relating Cadillac's role in creating and reflecting American culture through the smooth, and even the rough, periods of its history. And with the current excitement rumbling through Cadillac, there appear to be smooth straight-aways in the company's future.

A book-writing journey is never a solo adventure, and I owe many thanks to friends and peers who helped make this book a pleasure and an educational experience to write. First, thanks to Krause Publications book publisher Bill Krause for trusting a young soul like myself to undertake such a great task, and to *Old Cars Weekly* editorial director Keith Mathiowetz and previous *Old Cars Weekly* editorial director John Gunnell for believing that I could complete this book. Tooling through a book such as this would be nothing without the scenery, so a grand thank-you must go to the people who helped furnish unpublished photos to make this book the visual feast that it is. Robert Maidment put photos into my hands from Great Britain; Fellow Cadillac LaSalle Club Int. members opened their garages and closed their shutters to supply fountains of Cadillac and LaSalle photos for this project; Gregg D. Merksamer and John Adams-Graf opened their collections to offer more photos of Cadillacs; Jennifer Knightstep Lesniak of General Motors Media Archives helped me ruffle through the goldmine of images housed in General Motors' archives; Ron Kowalke for providing photo leads for this book; Tom Bartsch and Brian Earnest for providing their editing expertise; and to Ryan Gilman for providing a few laughs and equal friendship when I needed them.

The pleasures of driving this 1962 Coupe deVille, which I bought eight years ago when I was 19, helped keep my inspiration high while writing this book.

Foreword

The history of Cadillac is filled with performance, style, and most importantly, passion. From the glamorous early days with V-12 and V-16 engines, through the eras of big cars and tail fins, there has always been enough power and polish to captivate car lovers from all over the world.

In the late 1990s, after a period that was not the strongest in Cadillac's history, General Manager John Smith began to execute a plan to restore Cadillac to the top of any list. Originally dubbed Art and Science, the vision portrayed a bold new styling vocabulary, leading performance and technology, and a return to obvious passion for both.

Part of changing the perception of the public was a return to racing! Behind the scenes, in addition to great designs for the street, a program was underway to take Cadillac up against the world's best at the 24 Hours of Le Mans. The Cadillac Le Mans Prototype raced for top honors at Le Mans, and around the U.S. in the American Le Mans Series, against the best from Audi, Bentley, and Porsche.

Though the program never captured a coveted race win, the effort was a success on two fronts. Cadillac had proven that its vision for change was much more than words, and had shown that its target was again to be judged the best in the world.

Le Mans has a strong global audience, but by 2002 Cadillac's focus was made even sharper—to concentrate on U.S. sales growth. The Le Mans Prototype program was cancelled, to the disappointment of many newly made race fans.

But the vision is still being realized, and a new Cadillac racing program will be born in 2004. This one, destined for U.S. road racing tracks, will again bring Cadillac up against Audi, BMW, and Porsche.

Watch for the new CTS-V race car, and watch as Cadillac writes the next chapter in its story.

David Spitzer
Team Cadillac

100 Years

Contents

History

The earliest Cadillacs were the automotive world's first rebels. They climbed the steps to government buildings; they tempted competitors in contests of speed and stamina; and they dared the early automobile establishment to match their innovation.

Cadillac founder Henry Leland was no rebel himself. He served his country during the Civil War by working as an expert mechanic at the Crompton-Knowles Loom Works at Springfield, Massachusetts, where he developed a Blanchard lathe used to manufacture gunstocks for Union soldiers. But with the end of the Civil War came the end of young Leland's career at the loom works, and from this point on all the steps in his career would be more like leaps.

100 Years

Leland found employment at the rapidly growing Colt revolver company, and he was a perfect fit with impeccable timing. Under the direction of Elisha A. Root, Colt had just invested unheard amounts of money in manufacturing equipment that improved the accuracy and precision of the company's weapons and, more importantly, their components. Leland's two-year stint at Colt helped him appreciate precision in the manufacturing process and sharpened his skills as a mechanic.

Colt had been a wise career move for Leland, but when he joined the famous precision machine builders Brown and Sharp only two years after joining Colt, Leland had reached the highest echelon of precision manufacturing. The reputation of Brown and Sharpe was unmatched, as was the precision of their

instruments that regularly measured tolerances of hundred-thousandths or even millionths of an inch. When Brown and Sharp switched from watch repair to precision tool manufacturing, the company became a household name and set new standards for quality. It is from this prosperity that its advertising slogan, "The World's Standard for Accuracy," grew. This slogan would soon apply to Leland's own projects.

The training he acquired at the premier manufacturing businesses couldn't have better prepared Leland for his next challenge, one that would lead him into automobile manufacture. By 1890, Leland was ready to move on, and through a Detroit contact he met Robert C. Faulconer. Together, Leland and Faulconer recognized the need for machining services in a growing Detroit, and using

The seed from which Cadillac sprouted. Alanson Brush, shown behind the wheel, is accompanied by Henry Leland's son, Wilfred, in this photo of the first Cadillac from late 1902. (GM Media Archives)

Faulconer's lumber fortunes, the pair founded Leland and Faulconer. Later that year, Leland and Faulconer was joined by Henry's son, Wilfred Leland, who had become a gifted mechanic in his own right under his father's instruction.

The company grew quickly, as did its reputation for castings and forgings. Beginning in 1896, the firm began to manufacture automobile engines and chassis components in the Detroit area.

The company's quality did not go unnoticed by local automobile manufacturers, least of all fellow Detroit manufacturer Ransom E. Olds. His familiarity with Leland and Faulconer led him to the steps of the company's Faulconer's Trombley Avenue plant in his search for a quieter transmission for his own motor car. Like other manufacturers of mechanical parts, Olds had been individually hand filing the gears to fit, causing obnoxious sounds from his transmission. Leland presented Olds with a silent, precision-ground transmission, whose parts were completely interchangeable from automobile to automobile.

A pleased Ransom Olds soon awarded Leland and Faulconer a contract to build 2,000 curved-dash Olds engines to their specs, although they weren't the only ones to receive the contract. The Dodge brothers, John and Horace, also received an equal contract to build identical engines for the Olds. However, the engines ended up being anything but identical. Each company manufactured the engines with its own technology, and testing proved the Leland unit to be superior in the power it exerted. This power advantage was mainly a byproduct of the car's smooth-operating, precision-ground parts.

The two engines were shown together at the first Detroit automobile show in 1901. They were displayed running side by side, at the same speed, but the Leland and Faulconer engine had a cheat brake to hinder its performance and curb its horsepower down to that of the Dodge brothers-built engine. The precision grinding of the Leland and Faulconer engine was credited with supplying 23 percent more horsepower than the inferior Dodge engine.

Inspired by the Detroit show, Leland set out to improve Oldsmobile's one-cylinder engine with the help of Leland and Faulconer engineers. In another brilliant move, Leland sent Charles Martens, head of Leland and Faulconer's engine testing department, to the Olds plant to monitor the company's design and manufacturing methods. Once there, Martens found that though Olds possessed knowledge of mechanical concepts, his methods could use fine tuning.

From the ashes of Henry Ford's second failed automobile company, Henry Leland, along with several investors, created the Cadillac Automobile Company. Leland is credited with forging the advancements that separated Cadillac from the hundreds of other automobile companies springing up at the beginning of the 20th century.

Representing Cadillac's first production model in the Cadillac Historical Collection is this 1903 Model A with a rear-entrance tonneau. The one-cylinder, 10-horsepower car has been owned by the Cadillac Historical Collection for several decades. (Cadillac Historical Collection)

Frederick Stanley Bennett was the first to take the Cadillac nameplate overseas as a distributor, doing so in 1903. At his urging, the Royal Automobile Club conducted the standardization test that earned Cadillac the right to pronounce its products as the "Standard of the World." Here, Bennett greets the drivers of the three Cadillacs that underwent the test. (Cadillac Historical Collection)

Henry Leland poses with the phone booth-like coupe he had built to test the feasibility of adding a closed Cadillac to the company's catalog. Leland drove the car daily, sometimes tipping it over, and his family reportedly had the car detuned to slow Henry down. Leland soon figured out his "Osceola," the name given to the car, had been tampered with and hopped up the one-cylinder engine beyond its original specifications. Leland never sold the prototype, and his family eventually donated it to the Cadillac Historical Collection, where it can be seen today. (GM Media Archives)

Cadillac earned the prestigious Dewar Trophy twice; the first, after three Cadillacs passed a rigorous parts standardization test by the Royal Automobile Club in 1908, and the second after the group exhaustively scrutinized Cadillac's self-starting system in 1912. The first awarding of the Dewar Trophy inspired Cadillac to adopt the phrase "Standard of the World" in its advertising. (Cadillac Historical Collection)

Paul A. Ianuario, Sr.'s 1908 Cadillac Model T tulip-bodied Victoria touring hails from the year in which Cadillac's standardization of parts was tested by the Royal Automobile Club.

The components from the disassembled 1908 single-cylinder Cadillacs were jumbled together and then reassembled by members of the Royal Automobile Club in the parts standardization test held between February 29 and March 13, 1908. (Cadillac Historical Collection)

Martens ran back to Leland and Faulconer with his observations and, working with Leland's engineers, improved upon the Olds design by increasing the valve diameter, exhaust passages and ports, as well as regrinding the cam. Of course, such improvements come at a cost. Expensive new toolings were needed to build the engine and increase the strength of the chassis to withstand the additional power of the Leland-designed power plant. It wasn't a price Olds was willing to pay, however, and Leland went home, disappointed (although his improved engine found a home in the family Olds).

Leland's disappointment didn't last long. On a summer afternoon in 1902, two investors, William Murphy and Lemuel Bowen, familiar with Leland and Faulconer's stellar reputation, settled into Henry's office with a request. The pair, looking to dissolve their investment in Henry Ford's three-year-old Henry Ford Company, wanted appraisal advice for the failed company's assets. While he was a part of the company, Ford did produce a few race cars, including the 999 race car, but Murphy and Bowen understood that profits would come from a road car, not race cars.

Leland agreed to look over the Henry Ford Company's remains, but upon doing so, imagined new potential for the company's assets. Rather than liquidate the company, Leland suggested that his improved engine could breath new life into the company. Leland convinced Murphy and Bowen that his engine would be their salvation for two reasons: It was more powerful than the Olds power plant, and it was far more reliable. His latter point was especially appealing in a time when an-ill behaved horse could be favorable to a moody automobile.

Once the investors' laughter subsided, they accepted Leland's recommendation, and on August 22, 1902, the reorganized company was christened "Cadillac" after the European founder of the company's Detroit hometown. Not long after, engineer Alanson Brush drove the first completed car carrying the Cadillac name on October 17, 1902.

Early automobile manufacture is incestuous, and many players' names keep popping up like on an old boys' club roster, so it's not surprising both the name of the driver of the first Cadillac, Brush, and the Model A model name of the car he piloted would return, though in each case on cars carrying names other than Cadillac.

Murphy and Bowen recognized Leland's leadership possibilities in the revitalized company, and with fellow investors, placed Leland in a position of considerable power on the board of directors. He was also given stock in the new company. The Leland and Faulconer business was also not forgotten in the new enterprise, and the company was to go on building Leland's one-cylinder engines, as well as transmissions and steering gears for the car, while another converted plant was to provide the Cadillac's body and chassis components.

The first run of cars was small, but two of them followed Cadillac's first sales manager, sales wizard William E. Metzger, to the New York Auto Show in January of 1903. Metzger proved his sales prowess at the show, selling out the entire expected first run well before the show ended. Of course, much of Metzger's success should be credited to Leland, who made the car an appealing horseless carriage to the small automobile-hungry class.

The 1911 Model Thirty displaced 286 cubic inches and carried a 32-horsepower rating. (GM Media Archives)

A buyer could expect to get a lot from this new kid on the block. Leland expected consistent perfection in the construction of the car and its components. Each piston perfectly fit into its cylinder cavity and, unlike other automobiles on the market, would perfectly fit into a fellow Cadillac's cylinder cavity without expensive machine work from a blacksmith. Such manufacturing allowed an owner to become his own mechanic, bringing the dawn of the shade tree mechanic. To do this, Leland carried over his precision engineering that dictated most parts were to be manufactured with tolerances less than 1/1000th of an inch. Other manufacturers would have happily used parts and tools that Leland demanded be scrapped.

Early Cadillacs gained a reputation of reliability and low maintenance, but all was not well. While the Cadillac's engine was known for its efficiency, power, and quiet operation, the remainder of the car suffered. Because it was far more powerful than its contemporaries, Leland's one-cylinder outperformed the chassis around it. Parts that were not Leland built or designed were failing, forcing the factory to make costly repairs. Returns caused by these inferior parts were doing nothing for the factory's efficiency, which had been further hindered by a devastating plant fire in 1904, and they only added to the frustration Cadillac-hungry customers experienced while they waited for their cars to roll off the infant assembly line.

Cadillac introduced the first mass-produced V-8 engine in a passenger car in 1915, and after a successful first year, the company chose not to mess with a good thing and incorporated only a few changes. Andy Flagge and Linda Scharf's 1916 Type 53 seven-passenger touring car benefited from an enlarged intake manifold and carburetor modifications to bring it up to 77 horsepower—a 10-percent increase from 1915. (Angelo Van Bogart photo)

This 1918 Type 57 Victoria Opera Coupe resides in the Cadillac Historical Collection. Features of the innovative car include its V-8 engine, an all-aluminum body, tilt-away steering wheel, and high/low beam headlamps actuated by mechanically shifting the positions of the reflectors inside each headlamp. (Cadillac Historical Collection)

Problems from a downed plant and a substandard chassis didn't stop Cadillac from outperforming anything around, however. In 1904, an inebriated driver was goaded by a dealer into propelling a hickory-spoked Cadillac up the steps of the Capitol building, replicating Alanson Brush's own step-climbing adventure with a chain-clad prototype on the steps of the Wayne County Building in 1902. Yet another Cadillac, this one weighed down with 16 passengers, was pictured in a 1904 copy of the Detroit Free Press climbing the city's Selby Hill. Highly publicized stunts helped offset any problems buyers had with the cars, and demand grew.

Perspective buyers looking to trade their horse-and-buggies for the latest in wheeled technology in 1904 got a maroon-painted Model A runabout with enough space for only two occupants for their well-earned $750. For the second year, Cadillac answered the public's demand for more space and made a rear tonneau available to those willing to add an additional $100 to the car's $750 base price. For $30 more, an optional buggy top would provide a bit of protection, at least from the sun.

Those who waited an additional year to join the combustion revolution saw the new Model B join the Model A in Cadillac's 1904 lineup. The two Cadillac models were sold alongside one another, and at the factory, their engines were built together. They shared the same one-cylinder engine, which had been down-rated to 8 1/4 hp from the 1903's 9.7 hp. But while the power plants were shared, the exteriors of the two were polar opposites for the time. The Model A continued to wear an attractive, albeit humble, design with a curved dashboard and the radiator tucked below. The Model B was more refined and reflected the path all car design was headed. Instead of bearing a radiator below its dashboard as its forward focal point, the new Model B received a hood forward of the passenger compartment.

The one-lunger continued to nestle itself beneath the front seat, so the Model B's hood provided a small luggage space in front of the driver. To accommodate this design change, the front-mounted radiator was turned from a horizontal position on the Model A to a vertical position on the Model B. Differences didn't end there, either. Whereas the Model A was of a runabout design that could be optioned out with a rear seat (or tonneau), the Model B came as either a four-passenger Surrey or as a two-passenger runabout without the option of adding a rear tonneau at a later time. While this design forced a buyer to make a permanent decision at purchase time, it did allow rear passengers in the four-passenger surrey easier access to their seat, since they could now enter from either side of the car.

Despite the April 13, 1904, fire disaster, young Cadillac had a good sales year. A healthy 2,418 cars had been sold, thanks to a work force that operated under a six-day work week and with nights shifts. Despite faults with the non-Cadillac components, the company gained a reputation for performance and quality, and outside of the company's walls, few knew the production problems plaguing the automaker. It seemed as soon as the company squashed the bugs cropping up in returned units, production problems took them back two steps. A solution came from Murphy and Bowen on Christmas Eve, 1904, when they called on the Lelands to reorganize the relationships between Leland and Faulconer and the Cadillac Automobile Company. What emerged was a self-sufficient Cadillac Motor Car Company that would manufacture all of its own components. Murphy and Bowen entrusted Henry M. Leland with the renewed enterprise and named him general manager.

With Leland in charge, Cadillac was better prepared to break into the new luxury car market. Cadillac took its first step into the upscale automobile market with its $2,800 Model D. In both price and size, the car dwarfed its little-changed Model B and its new Models E and F sister cars. While new in name and styling, the Models E and F were refined cars that continued use of the Model B's dummy hood and radiator arrangement and the trustworthy one-lung Cadillac engine. The Model D, on the other hand, quadrupled the cylinder count with a thoroughly tested four-cylinder engine that emerged after the company had tested several different two-, three-, and four-cylinder engines.

With 30 hp coming from its 301-cid four-cylinder, the Model D had lots of power for the time. After passing through the rear door and climbing up into the Cadillac Model D's rear seat, passengers could count on reaching speeds of up to 50 mph. If the car's buyer didn't elect to pay extra for a top, it could be a very windy 50 mph.

Price kept the Model D from competing with its moderately priced siblings, and the less-extravagant Cadillacs gained prestige from sharing a nameplate with the high-end Model D. With tales of stair-climbing adventures and high society rolled up on newsprint under their arms, a car shopper could examine a Cadillac and know it was the best car for his money, whether he spent $2,800 on a D, or $780 on an E. By the end of the year, the company hit the 8,000-car mark. Some 3,712 cars rolled out of the Detroit plant in 1905 alone (including 156 four-cylinder Model D's and 3,556 one-cylinder B's, E's, and F's), all of them carrying the coat of arms of Le Sieur Antoine de la Mothe, the French explorer who founded the city that was Cadillac's home, and all of them continuing the precision-ground engineering processes that made them superior automobiles for the time.

Cadillac served its country well by supplying thousands of touring cars, like this 1918 Type 57 seven-passenger touring, and a smaller number of limousines to the United States government for use in World War I. (John Adams-Graf collection)

Cadillac had an exciting year in 1926: the company moved into its Clark Street administration building; Lawrence P. Fisher became Cadillac's general manager; Harley Earl was commissioned to design a new junior Cadillac; and the company had an all-new Series 314 line for the 1926 model year. This Series 314 Custom Coupe for five passengers was priced at $4,000. (GM Media Archives)

Despite the V-8-powered Series 355's greater sales, the V-16 received all of the glory in 1930, quickly followed by the scene-stealing V-12 announcement in 1931. In 1931, Cadillac sold 10,700 V-8-powered automobiles, only slightly less than the previous year, despite the worsening Depression. (GM Media Archives)

While the four-cylinder Model D gets most of the attention, despite its rarity compared to the one-cylinder models, there is a single 1905 model that stands alone. That car is Henry Leland's personal car, nicknamed "Old Plug Hat," and better known today as "Osceola." The little blue-and-black coupe's creation was ordered by Leland as a sort of test bed for the possible addition of closed cars to the Cadillac lineup. Built under supervision of Fred J. Fisher at Detroit's Wilson °Body Company, 82-inch-tall Osceola became Henry Leland's personal car for at least five years. The car eventually wound up on the Leland family grounds until it was revived for the movie screen and the 1933 and 1934 Chicago World's Fairs. Its popularity in these venues encouraged the Leland family to share the

car with the public, and after spending time in a small string of museums, it now calls the Cadillac Historical Collection home.

The telephone booth-like Osceola was endearing to Henry Leland, and the body style earned a position near the top of the Cadillac lineup in 1906. A gargantuan $3,000 price tag brought buyers not only protection from the elements, it did it with class and style. Buyers could watch for horses and road ruts through beveled window glass. Window draperies hung from the rear window. Most Cadillac buyers, and there were many, opted for the far-less-expensive four-cylinder models, which continued to be consecutively lettered.

This attractive 1931 Cadillac Series 355 coupe features several Cadillac accessories, including a heron hood ornament, metal side-mount covers, side-mount mirrors, and wind-wing window vents. (GM Media Archives)

Prices also remained consistent through the years, and still started at $750 for the one-cylinder Model K Light Runabout. Coincidentally, that hefty sum was the salary each Leland earned per month; Wilfred for his work as assistant treasurer under initial financier William H. Murphy, and Henry for his position as general manager.

The Lelands were worth every penny, as proven by the 14,000 single-cylinder Cadillac models biting through America's dirt roads by 1906. Adding to that total was 1906's healthy output of 3,559 cars, most of which were one-cylinder models. Cadillac could tout that it had the best-equipped (and largest) automobile factory in the world.

After receiving the okay of the United States Patent Office, the company was also able to christen its cars with the family coat-of-arms of its namesake, Le Sieur Antoine de la Mothe Cadillac, by the August of 1906. Although a variation of this crest had appeared as early as 1904 on some Cadillacs, the coronet-crowned and laurel wreath-cradled coat of arms became the official property of the company and is still seen on Cadillac products.

If 1906 was Cadillac's peak production year during the company's infancy, then 1907 was a fall down the other side of the slope. Demand for Cadillac's one-cylinder gem was still present, but the effects of six-cylinder offerings from competitors was taking a toll on sales, which fell 37 percent in 1907. For the first time, the one-cylinder Cadillac, now identified as the Model K, saw a price increase of $50, to $800. It was only available as a two-seat runabout. More seating arrangements for single-cylinder-powered Cadillacs were found in the Model M lineup, which included a touring car, a Victoria, a folding rear tonneau, and a straight-lined standard tourer. Closed bodies on the Model M chassis included an Osceola-style coupe and a delivery vehicle.

Increased competition among quality, six-cylinder cars was keeping the Lelands on their toes, and to compete in this mid-priced market, Cadillac brought out the Model G in 1907. Priced between the bargain ($1,000) one-cylinder K's and M's and the spendy four-cylinder Model H ($3,600) limousines and giant touring cars, the new $2,000 Model G was a medium-powered four-cylinder with a medium price.

Adding the Model G to the lineup was key to Cadillac's survival, but it didn't compare to the moves stirring in the building's walls in 1908. In one small block of time, Cadillac cemented itself as the standard by which other automobile companies would compare themselves. The company also integrated itself into a

The glow from the Steel Pier in Atlantic City reveals a 1931 Cadillac Series 370A coupe, at left, and a 1931 Chevrolet Independence Series AE sport coupe, at right. (GM Media Archives)

union of automobile companies, ultimately helping the company persevere through coming hard times. When not in these other pursuits, Cadillac also created an entirely new car to carry the company into the next decade.

By 1908, the time had come to retire Cadillac's one-cylinder cars. Their successful reign had created a foundation that established the company as a quality producer of reliable automobiles, and this fact hadn't gone unnoticed around the world, specifically by London Cadillac importer Frederick S. Bennett. In 1903, Bennett brought the first Cadillac to Great Britain, and spent years convincing customers of his Anglo-American Motor Car Company of London that the Cadillac was as good a car as the French and German products many thought to be superior. Bennett was ready to test this ideology by 1908 and challenged Britain's prestigious Royal Automobile Club to test the one-cylinder Cadillac's merits with an interchangeability contest. Other automobile manufacturers were still practicing the hand-fitting of parts in their automobiles, and the club was justifiably intrigued by the proposition. By February 29,1908, three single-cylinder Cadillacs were plucked from a loading dock. The club then supervised each car's 23-mile trip from the dock to the new Brooklands Metrodome track and witnessed the cars complete 10 laps before being locked up for the disassembly.

As few as two and possibly as many as six Royal Automobile Club mechanics from its technical committee tore the Cadillac runabouts apart and jumbled their combined 6,489 parts together over three days in early March. Bennett added another miscellaneous 89 parts from his dealer stock to further prove the interchangeability of the components. During the cars' downtime, water filled their storage spaces and added a light rust covering to the parts. With a mild cleaning and without any filing or other manipulation that other manufacturers regularly practiced when building new cars, the cars were re-assembled and prepared for what would be an industry-shaking event. After adding oil, fuel, and topping off the cars' water levels, testers fired up the cars before an audience and then drove them back to the Brooklands Metrodome for the ultimate test of Leland's manufacturing philosophy.

An even 500 miles later, with several Cadillac officials looking on, Leland's thorough technique was proven. Without any glitches, the one-cylinders averaged 34 mph while spinning around the track. Though considered outdated, the six-year-old one-cylinders provided their final triumph to their creator before being replaced by a new Cadillac.

Following a final inspection, the prestigious Royal Automobile Club presented Cadillac with its "Certificate of Performance" on March 13, 1908, and the

A V-12 roadster was selected for pacemaking duties, but a Cadillac V-16 dual-cowl phaeton was selected as the official car of the Indianapolis 500 in 1931. Bill Rader is behind the wheel. (GM Media Archives)

Although the Series 61 and Series 62 Cadillacs flaunted fresh styling, they shared the assembly line with the little-changed Fleetwood Series 75 models. Here, a Series 61 Cadillac coupe precedes a Fleetwood 75 at the end of the assembly line at Cadillac's Clark Street plant. (GM Media Archives)

European accolades didn't end there. Sir Thomas Dewar presented Cadillac with his coveted Dewar Trophy, a giant silver cup, for the heralded achievement. It would be the only time an American automobile manufacturer would receive the honor. The issuing of the Dewar Trophy earned Cadillac widespread media coverage and provided the company with an opportunity to spread its new, and well-earned, motto "Standard of the World" throughout its advertising.

Before Cadillac underwent this test, automobile company assimilator William Crapo Durant approached Leland about selling his company to Durant's growing General Motors conglomeration. Leland set a firm price of $3.5 million in cash, a sum which exceeded Durant's offer by $500,000. When Durant approached Leland again only six months later, Leland had raised the price to $4.1 million, and again Durant passed. It would be an expensive mistake for him. A third, and final, offer was made to Leland following the awarding of the "Certificate of Performance," and Leland accepted. By the time the paperwork settled in 1909, Durant had dug deep from the coffers of GM's Buicks division to pay Leland a total of $5.6 million; $500,000 in cash and the remainder in GM preferred stock. The sale made headlines as the biggest transaction the Detroit Stock Exchange had ever seen.

With the production disasters of 1904 still fresh in everyone's minds, Durant agreed that the Lelands and their management team would continue to run Cadillac as if they still owned the company. This fluidity of leadership certainly aided the smooth transition to Cadillac's new Model Thirty at the end of 1908. Gone were the hyper-expensive Model H limousine, the middle-of-the-road Model G, and the trusted one-cylinders, which had followed the alphabet up to Models S and T. Cadillac was back to a single-model lineup for 1909, and the buying public enthusiastically swallowed up the company's Model Thirty. There were only three models to choose from—a roadster, a demi-tonneau, and a touring car—but loyal customers didn't mind. In the first six months, Cadillac had orders for 4,500 cars, a number surpassing every other model-year's production total. By year's end, Cadillac produced an incredible 5,900 cars, all undergoing Leland's strict fit-and-finish practice and all priced at $1,400.

The Model Thirty was a huge success, but it wasn't an entirely new car. The four-cylinder engine and the easy-to-service and customer-accepted selective sliding gear transmission were borrowed from the previous year's Model G, though power increased from 20 horsepower to an advertised 25.6 horsepower. Cadillac dynamometer testing actually revealed a 30-horsepower rating, hence the new car's name, but the factory stuck to its lower rating. Because nearly every part on the Model Thirty was made in-house, Cadillac was able to keep the cost of the Model Thirty in the one-cylinder's mid-priced category. Buyers were happy, as were stockholders upon realizing 24-percent dividends from the $25 profit Cadillac made per car.

The key word at Cadillac in 1910 was "more." More choices, more power, and more cars, all despite a base price that was $200 more than 1909's $1,400 starting price on similar models. And buyers were willing to pay it. They also received more car for their money. Wheelbases on the touring car, demi-tonneau, roadster (now called a Gentleman's Roadster), and a revived closed coupe were all up to 110 inches, four inches more than the 106-inch wheelbase found on the 1909 Model Thirty. Curiously, 150 new $2,200 Osceola-style coupe bodies were ordered by Henry Leland from the two-year-old Fisher Body Company of Detroit, marking the start of a relationship between General Motors and the Fisher brothers' young shop.

After a one-year absence, a factory-assembled limousine was available for wealthy Cadillac buyers. To offer the level of comfort and room one would expect in a premier automobile, Cadillac gave the limousine a 120-inch wheelbase. Power for all models, including the limousine, came from the same larger-for-1910 four-cylinder engine that now displaced 255.3 cid and a higher 28.9 advertised horsepower rating (though factory testing on the dynamometer revealed the output was 33 horsepower).

A taste of new technology came with Charles F. Kettering's DELCO ignition system. Not to be confused with the self starter, Kettering's sets still required a magneto to fire the four-cylinder Cadillac engine. Leland ordered 8,000 DELCO sets in 1909 from Kettering for Cadillac's 1910 models. Like his dealings with the Fisher brothers, Leland's purchase from Kettering started a relationship that continues to this day.

An amazing 8,008 Cadillacs were cranked out of the Detroit plant in 1910, but the same success was not being realized in the recently formed GM conglomeration, and Leland's business acumen came to the rescue. Just as he had saved the remains of one of Henry Ford's failed business ventures and turned it into the booming Cadillac Motor Car Company, Leland stopped the dissolution of General Motors when the overextended William Durant was forced out of the company.

Wowing crowds with engineering feats had never been a problem for Cadillac, but when jaws dropped at New York's 1910 National Automobile Show, it wasn't what was under the hood that had them in awe. That year, Cadillac unveiled its new "Torpedo," a sleek touring car that gently smoothed out some

Cadillac was selected to pace the Indianapolis 500-Mile Race in 1932 with a brilliant white V-12 roadster with silver striping and matching white upholstery. Cadillac test driver Bill Rader commanded the Cadillac around the track and is seen here in a similar V-12 roadster, which may be the pace car before a repaint. (GM Media Archives)

Nicholas Dreystadt's efforts to reduce costs at Cadillac after his 1934 appointment to the general manager position probably saved Cadillac from extinction.

*Cadillac General Manager
Nicholas Dreystadt, third from
right, and Chevrolet-Pontiac
President William S.
Knudsen, fourth from right,
greet the new 1934 Cadillacs
and LaSalles as they come off
the assembly line. They are
accompanied by the Fisher
brothers. (GM Media
Archives)*

A line of 1936 Cadillacs, led by a convertible sedan, roll off the assembly line at the Clark Street plant. (GM Media Archives)

of the traditional horseless carriage design cues with a package that was clearly more modern. The Torpedo's hood blended into the cowl; its sides grew taller for a more enclosed feel; and its edges and flanks grew ribs. While certainly not the outright styling coup d'etat the Osceola had been, the body style exuded a certain grace not found on other cars. Excited crowds told Cadillac to build it, and the company listened, adding the Torpedo model for the 1911 model year.

The Torpedo may have grabbed all of the attention, but there were other visible exterior changes in the Model Thirty lineup. Touring cars were popular with customers, so it was not surprising that when Cadillac added a second new model, the Fore-Door Tourer, it also followed the basic characteristics of the touring car. Model Thirty touring cars in previous years had rear-opening doors only, so when Cadillac chose a name for its new touring car with opening front doors, it cleverly chose the "Fore-Door" name.

With the model lineup once again crowding, Cadillac dropped the demi-tonneau model at the end of the year. It, and the rest of the lineup (excepting the limousine), used a 6-inch-longer wheelbase, but only the sharpest Cadillac shoppers noticed the 116-inch hub-to-hub distance. To help pull the additional weight of the longer wheelbase, Cadillac engineers increased the horsepower to 32 units by squaring the engine's bore and stroke to an equal 4 1/2 inches for each. Total displacement was now 286.3 inches.

After three years, the Thirty designation vanished, but it's likely few noticed as the entire industry was blinded by Cadillac's electrifying new device—the self starter. Thanks to Charles Kettering, who had developed an electric ignition system for use in 1910 Cadillacs, a driver no longer had to spin a crank nosing its way out from beneath a Cadillac grille. Using the knowledge he gained from developing an electric crank for cash registers, Kettering created an electric system through his Dayton Engineering Laboratories Company (DELCO) that produced a quick electric charge that, simply stated, duplicated the hand cranking motion on an automobile. Gone from this system was the magneto that Kettering initially used on the starting system he developed earlier for Cadillac.

The technological triumph did not go unnoticed by the motoring press or the Royal Automobile Club, which once again exhaustively tested the innovation in more than 1,000 repeated starting and stopping trials. The Cadillac didn't blink, and was again awarded the Dewar Trophy for the magnificent mechanical conquest. By winning, Cadillac maintained its position as the only American automobile manufacturer to ever win the coveted Dewar Trophy, even since 1912, and the only manufacturer in the world to ever receive it twice.

Bob Murphy's 1937 LaSalle represents the first year a Cadillac-built engine returned between the LaSalle's front fenders. Between 1934 and 1936, all LaSalles were powered by an Oldsmobile-built engine manufactured to Cadillac's specifications.

Sales of 1937 Cadillacs were twice those of the previous year. Adam Schoolsky's 1937 Cadillac Series 75 convertible sedan helped contribute to the increase through its showing at the 1936 New York National Auto Show.

With V-8 power and Cadillac reliability, LaSalle and Cadillac chassis were popular among professional car coachbuilders. This restored 1939 LaSalle carries a Woodbridge Emergency Squad plaque above its front bumper and was restored by members of that organization.

By the LaSalle's final year, 1940, its headlights sank into the front fenders, as on other 1940 General Motors automobiles, and like the rest of the industry, sealed-beam headlamps were used. Marshall E. Lamenzo's 1940 LaSalle convertible coupe is from the premium LaSalle line introduced mid-year that uses General Motors' sleek torpedo body shell.

With World War II raging, Cadillac's 1942 model year was abbreviated, but the public would have a chance to pick up a pontoon-fendered Cadillac at war's end with warmed-over versions of the restyled 1942 models in 1946 and 1947. Arthur and Marge Swanson's rare Series 62 Sedanette is one of 1,045 fastbacks built on the longer 129-inch wheelbase in 1942. (Angelo Van Bogart photo)

A line of coveted 1946 Cadillacs are shown passing through heat lamps used to dry the freshly applied paint. (GM Media Archives)

Abandoned were the gas generator and old acetylene headlamps, which were replaced by the superior Gray and Davis electrical headlamps. Each Cadillac speedometer became lit for night driving, sharing a power source with an electrically illuminated taillight and a pair of cowl-mounted lamps. Kettering's self-starting device took women out of the passenger seat and eliminated dangerous hand cranking. So revolutionary was the design that every other car became instantly outdated, even those cars beyond the Cadillac's own mid-price bracket. Cadillac was rewarded by the public with 13,995 sales in the 1912 model year, and Kettering was eventually rewarded with an executive position in General Motors, but that was a few years and several patents away.

Overshadowed by the company's technological innovations was the 1912 disappearance of the demi-tonneau and the touring car model without front doors. In their place came a new, four-passenger touring car. Meanwhile, sporting types enjoyed the new aesthetics of the restyled roadster and chauffers were treated to the completely enclosed berline limousine. But it was what was

under the hood that again earned Cadillac the most attention for the 1913 model year.

A gigantic increase in the displacement of the Cadillac four-cylinder brought the size up to 365.8 cubic inches and horsepower to 48.7 impressive units. To turn this engine over more efficiently, Kettering's self starter and the accompanying lighting system were both mildly improved. Those judging the Cadillac by its skin noticed a new rear deck on the recently restyled roadster and the addition of yet another open Cadillac, a six-passenger open model. The "Six Passenger Car" provided one additional seat over the still-available five-passenger touring car at a $100 premium.

Buying time became the name of the game in 1914, as the company secretly began work on another industry-turning development with an entirely new power plant—the V-8 engine. But buying time didn't mean the company froze improvement measures. An early form of the swing-away steering wheel in a new left-side location made accessing the driver's seat easier. Cars from the

1914 model year can also be discerned from the previous year by their new demountable wheels and rear-mounted gas tank. Mechanically inclined collectors can look for the one-year-only two-speed rear axle that the company declared provided a 42-percent increase in speed with the flick of an electric dash-mounted switch.

Never one to follow, Cadillac was ready to share its well-kept secret for the 1915 model year and dazzled the industry with a new engine that changed the rules. The V-8 revelation was the result of a small engineering group's secret work out of a suburban Mount Clemens, Michigan, garage.

For at least two years, the engineering group had been hard at work on the engine. Previously, the eight-cylinder power plants were reserved for the most costly hand-built cars available only to the elite. Cadillac changed that with a single announcement in September of 1914, when it proclaimed it would be the first, and only, manufacturer to offer a mass-produced V-8. From the roadster to the limousine, every Cadillac would derive power from a 90-degree, V-type eight-cylinder engine that developed 70 horsepower from 314 cubic inches of displacement. The eight also incorporated an improved radiator, and a water-

cooling system that surpassed anything available on other hand-built eight-cylinder automobiles, including the luxurious Pierce-Arrow. Though little changed on the outside, the new power plant warranted a new designation to the entire lineup: Model 51. Rather than propel the car to the stratospheric price range of hand-built, V-8-powered cars like the Pierce-Arrow, Cadillac maintained its mid-range price, and for as little as $1,975, a buyer could slide themselves behind the wheel of the most innovative automobile available to them.

Despite tomato-throwing ad copy from competitors, the public excitedly embraced the new power plant and unashamedly bought up 13,000 V-8 Cadillacs in the engine's first year. The car's wild success can be attributed, at least partially, to the public's trust in Henry Leland's engineering methods, but design work on the V-8 must also be credited to Cadillac's chief designer, D. McCall White. A Scotsman who had previously worked at Daimler and Napier, White built for Cadillac a smooth, quiet engine that would kick up dust while cruising at speeds in excess of 55 mph. Few other cars could claim that kind of performance, and none with Cadillac reliability.

The original owners of this Antoinette Blue 1947 Cadillac Series 62 convertible either hit the top of a long waiting list early, or knew someone important at Capitol Cadillac in Washington, D.C., the place where this car was sold new, in order to receive delivery of their new Cadillac that year. More than 96,000 orders went unfilled by the end of 1947 as orders for new Cadillacs exceeded the available supply following the lean war years. Today, Bob and Grace Gluck own this handsome vehicle.

Along with performance, sales rose in 1916 to an incredible 18,000-unit high. These new Cadillacs, dubbed "Model 53s," featured a 10-percent horsepower increase, thanks to a few carburetor changes and an enlarged intake manifold. For the first time, it took more than $2,000 to pick up the least-expensive Cadillac model, the speedy two-seat roadster, from the company's Detroit docks. The roadster shared its $2,080 base price with the five-passenger touring car, dubbed the "Salon."

As Cadillac pressed out cars to meet demand, luxury car company and eventual Cadillac competitor Packard proclaimed the arrival of its Twin Six, the first mass-produced 12-cylinder automobile in the world. By the end of the year, the two companies would, ironically, find a tie between them and several other automobile manufacturers in a call to government service. Packard's 12-cylinder was found to be just what the government was looking for to power its wartime aircraft, but the automobile company was not to be alone in its manufacture. Ford, Packard, Nordyke and Marmon (builders of the Marmon automobile),

Buick, and Cadillac were among the companies granted contracts to build the 12-cylinder engine designed by Packard chief engineer Jesse Vincent and E. J. Hall of the Hall Scott Motor Company. Although the pair borrowed many design principles from other engine manufacturers, a completed test engine was delivered only six weeks after the project was launched.

The arrival of the contract to build these Liberty 12-cylinders in 1917 coincided with the return of General Motors founder William C. Durant to the company's helm. Like many Americans, Durant questioned U.S. involvement in The Great War. He also returned with a new attitude towards the Lelands' control of the operation of the GM subsidiary and immediately started butting heads with the patriotic pair.

Displeased, the Lelands left to form their Lincoln Company, and they made their first duty the production of 6,000 Liberty aircraft engines—the same number Packard was commissioned to produce. Cadillac eventually built only

1949 was a grand year to mark the monumental achievement of building 1,000,000 cars, and there wasn't a better car to be given the special honor than Cadillac's new two-door hardtop model, the Coupe deVille. The year also marked the introduction of the ultra-modern, 90-degree, overhead-valve V-8 engine. (GM Media Archives)

Briggs Cunningham entered two cars in the 1950 24 Hours of Le Mans, one a heavily modified Cadillac based on the Series 61 chassis, the other a relatively stock Series 61 coupe. Nicknamed "Le Monstre" by the press for its ungainly styling, the modified entry finished right behind the Series 61 coupe to take the 11th overall position. An unfortunate encounter with a sandy ditch hindered the modified Cadillac's success, but its finish was considered highly respectable regardless. (Cadillac Historical Collection)

2,000 Liberty aircraft, but its products found an additional calling to land battlefield duty. It was an arena Cadillac would dominate. Other countries understood Cadillac reliability and performance and employed the service of the company's motor cars in combat. Today, many Cadillac touring cars can be found in the time-worn pages of World War I veterans' photo albums.

At home, the U.S. Army tested several domestic automobiles for possible service and found the V-8 Cadillac to be superior after subjecting the cars to a grueling series of shake downs. The result was the shipment of more than 2,000 Cadillacs to the war front, in addition to those already ordered by foreign governments.

After the laughing subsided, the Le Monstre earned Cadillac much respect from spectators and fellow racers. (Cadillac Historical Collection)

Estimates of the number of Cadillacs sent overseas vary greatly. According to the Assistant Secretary of War, Director of Munitions Benedict Crowell's munitions report following World War I, 4,013 Cadillac touring cars and limousines were exported. Some of those became ambulances. A few even formed the basis of tank-like monstrosities while serving on war fronts, most notably French theaters. Other sources report as few as 2,095 Cadillacs found new homes in European battlefields and command centers. One thing is clear: Nothing beat a Cadillac. The United States Marine Corps agreed, and followed the Army's suit by naming the Cadillac touring model its official car.

The 1917 models were officially dubbed Type 55s, following the pattern of adding two to the previous year's designation since the first V-8 Type 51s of 1915. Revisions to the V-8 in 1917 were limited to lighter hourglass-shaped pistons that reduced friction, but a new, longer 125-inch wheelbase chassis wore a variety of new bodies. A four-passenger coupe and phaeton and a seven-passenger convertible touring car that provided both closed- and open-car versatility were added on the 125-inch-wheelbase chassis. The long, 132-inch-

wheelbase limousine chassis hosted a new Cadillac Laundaulet that featured a collapsible roof for rear passengers. The body style was often found in the catalogs of custom body builders, but Cadillac built its own for discriminating, and wealthy, buyers. Building its own exotic bodies similar to those offered by custom outfits would be a trend Cadillac would carry through the hey day of coach building. All Cadillac models were identifiable as 1917 models by their new crowned fenders and black enamel headlights.

Airplanes were in demand during WWI, and the Fisher brothers stepped up by fulfilling an aircraft contract awarded by the U.S. government. Manufacturing of the machines required that a new plant be built, and by 1918, the Fishers were in business. The brothers' company was purchased by General Motors in 1919, and over several decades, cranked out millions of Cadillac bodies.

Cadillac was not sitting down during the war, and in fact continued improving its product for the home front. An improved transmission and new, detachable heads for the otherwise unchanged V-8 could be found beneath a taller hood that reached back to a redesigned cowl area. Additional clearance for the engine was afforded by a taller radiator that marked 1918's newly designated Type 57 models. Customers were not intimidated by the changes to their trusted Cadillacs and put renewed faith in the cars they counted on by driving off in 20,000 of the revised Cadillacs. Even more Type 57s would be built upon the end of the conclusion of World War I, but the automotive business would soon understand what it meant to saturate the market.

There just weren't enough jobs for the thousands of returning soldiers. Despite the poor economic environment, Cadillac pumped out an impressive 19,628 cars in 1920, leaving most other automobile manufacturers envious of its prosperity. The quantity is even more impressive when the startling $785 price increase of the least-expensive two-passenger roadster and four-passenger touring car is taken into account. For a Cadillac driver to experience the feeling of wind blowing through his hair, they had to shell out $3,590 for the base-priced roadster or touring car.

Gun smoke clouds may have settled the previous year in Europe, but they were present in GM's management headquarters in 1920 as William C. Durant was ousted from power for the last time. But though Leland may have been gone from the Cadillac chain of command, but he wasn't out of its hair. In 1920, he returned to the field of automotive manufacture with a quality car named after his hero, Abraham Lincoln. Leland went with what was familiar and planted a V-8 on the chassis of his new creation in hopes of going head to head with the newly named Type 59 Cadillac of 1920. He proclaimed his car to be the "finest automobile made in the U.S.A." In a twist of irony, Leland sold the company to Henry Ford, the man whose own automobile company didn't succeed until Leland himself took control and turned it into Cadillac. Henry Ford and his son, Edsel, turned Lincoln into one of Cadillac's largest competitors.

Rough times faced Cadillac and the rest of the automobile industry as the nation fell into a depression following the return of troops from European

Because the company was organized at the end of 1902, Cadillac marked its 50th anniversary in 1952. Nancy DiTommaso's 1952 Series 62 sedan has been restored to a level befitting Cadillac's 50 years of accomplishment.

For comfortable motoring, this 1953 Cadillac Fleetwood Sixty Special sports air conditioning. The vents just ahead of the rear wheels are a tell-tale sign. (GM Media Archives)

battlefields. After enjoying prosperous times, Cadillac found itself not only in competition with other automakers, but itself. Along with the returning soldiers of World War I came an influx of used Cadillacs employed by the government as staff cars. With the shortfall of jobs for the now greatly increased workforce, homebound touring cars and limousines made 1920 a difficult year to sell new cars, and Cadillac failed to cross the 20,000-car mark as it had the previous two years.

Management changes swept through General Motors' premium brand. In his thirst to expand the GM empire, Durant had overextended the resources of the company. The drama may have actually benefited the company as it forced a reorganization, spearheaded by Alfred P. Sloan, who devised a line and staff management plan that would "eventually make General Motors Corporation the largest and most successful business enterprise in the world," according to Walter P. McCall in his excellent book, *80 Years of Cadillac LaSalle*. By 1923, Sloan would become president of General Motors and fully implement his plan to make each division function as an individual company.

The beginning of the Roaring Twenties also new brought competition that would challenge Cadillac through the remainder of the century. The source of the new luxury car competition came from Cadillac's own founder, Henry M. Leland. With his son, Wilfred, Henry set up shop across town to build the Lincoln motor car.

Further changes affected Cadillac's production and leadership the next year, 1921. New President and General Manager Herbert H. Rice became the leading man at Cadillac, and Earnest W. Seaholm was named Cadillac's chief engineer. The ongoing economic woes and Cadillac's move to the 2.5 million-square-foot Clark Avenue plant hurt new car sales, and only slightly more than 11,000 cars were built. The eight-building compound was so huge, many employees compared the plant to a self-sufficient city, and from it would come some of the finest and most memorable automobiles the world has ever seen.

The smoothness built into Cadillac's new-for-1924 V-8 engine marked the start of a Cadillac trademark that continues to this day. Credit for the silky operation should be attributed to the engine's dynamically balanced, two-plane crankshaft that eliminated any secondary shaking from the power plant. Models powered by the engineering masterpiece were crowned with a new designation: V-63.

Photos often show the inside of Cadillac's Clark Street plant in Detroit, Michigan, but few show the exterior. Here, an impressive line of 1955 Cadillacs is ready to be loaded below a giant Cadillac crest adorning a skyway between plant buildings. (GM Media Archives)

General Motors ruled the automotive industry throughout the 1950s, and part of its success was due to its consistent promotion of its products through such events as the Motorama. Several show cars cars can be seen of this aerial view of the floor at the 1955 Motorama. (GM Media Archives)

In a 1925 advertisement, Cadillac declared that more than 180,000 V-8s had been built, and not one of them had ever been replaced by the factory for any reason. Armed with a great engine, Cadillac Motor Car Division's new president, Lawrence P. Fisher, Jr., of Fisher Body Company, had the foundation to attain his new goal for Cadillac in 1925: Total dominance of the luxury car field. Tough competition for the role of "king of kings" came from established marques Packard, Pierce-Arrow, and Peerless, among others, but the rebounding economy of the 1920s welcomed the addition of a new player in the luxury car ranks.

Good timing and the addition of a lower-priced companion, the LaSalle, helped Cadillac beat its chief rival, Packard, which offered a fine series of eight-cylinder automobiles and an entry-level six-cylinder model. Styled by Don Lee and

Cadillac designer Harley Earl and fitted with its own 303-cid V-8, the colorful, two-tone LaSalle competed with Packard's junior six-cylinder model. As the first car to be designed by a designer rather than an engineer, the LaSalle would spark other future innovations that would add luster to the Cadillac division.

For 1929 models, the trademark smoothness of Cadillac, and now LaSalle, engines was matched by a new Synchro-Mesh Silent-Shift transmission that offered clashless shifting. Drivers no longer needed to double-clutch and gear changes were much smoother. The innovation was important, but it would be overshadowed by the stunning addition of the mighty V-16-powered cars at the end of the 1929.

Only upper levels of management were aware of what stylists and engineers had been concocting behind closed doors. Blueprints for designs labeled "coach" and "bus" kept outsiders in the dark as to Cadillac's developments with the V-16 engine, and since Cadillac had purchased the Fleetwood Body Co. in 1925, it was able to covertly prepare the special bodies for the magnificent chassis. When Cadillac's top-secret project was unveiled at the 1930 New York Auto Show, awe-struck visitors begged for information and photographs.

The Cadillac V-16s, dubbed "Series 452s" by the factory, enjoyed enormous, and somewhat unplanned, popularity in their first year. To meet demand, Cadillac stepped up production four times in the first year and built a total of 2,887 cars, with more than 2,500 sold. And just when the dust had finally settled after the V-16 announcement, Cadillac made a second announcement in June of 1930: It would add a V-12 power plant to its line of automobiles.

The move came despite the stock market crash of 1929 and the following Depression. The worsening economy would eventually hurt multi-cylinder Cadillac sales, but not before Cadillac squeezed out 5,725 V-12s by the end of the 1931 model year.

Enormous bites were being taken out of Cadillac's sales by 1932, but peering into a showroom, a window shopper would have had little clue. Fisher's plan to make yearly changes to Cadillac and LaSalle automobiles became evident on the outside of both automobiles in 1932 with more slippery designs that eliminated the grille screen and exposed frame sides and sills. Streamlining through skirted fenders and rounder body lines typified the 1933 models, and by 1934, LaSalle was again leading with design and engineering breakthroughs.

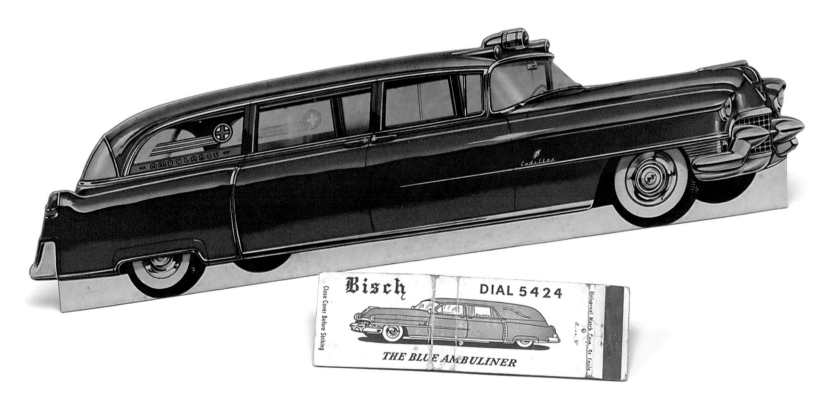

Cadillac-based ambulances and ambulance services were marketed in a variety of ways. Here, a matchbook touts Bisch's "blue ambulance" service. Also shown is a stand-up display promoting a Hess and Eisenhardt-built ambulance on the 1955 Cadillac chassis. (Kris Kandler/Bob Best photo)

Cadillac celebrated its milestones with class. This 1956 Cadillac Eldorado Biarritz was the 1,000,000th postwar Cadillac to roll off the assembly line. It took Cadillac 46 years to build the first million and only seven years to produce the second million. (GM Media Archives)

In a move to save the floundering LaSalle from extinction, Harley Earl and Jules Agramonte worked to design a stunning body that GM brass just couldn't say "no" to. Wowed by the LaSalle's tall, thin, race car-inspired grille and its high headlight pods mounted to the hood sides, General Motors management was unable to resist the Art Deco masterpiece. Advancements continued under the car with knee-action independent suspension and hydraulic brakes, and buyers responded by increasing their demand for the companion Cadillac model.

But it was a short victory. By 1940, the LaSalle nameplate would be gone from the Cadillac roster.

The devastating effects of The Depression began to lessen by 1936, and Cadillac was ready to make another bold move with the unveiling of two new luxurious automobiles—the beautifully styled Sixty Special, and the all-new V-16 series. The wonderful proportions and graceful styling of these cars energized the Cadillac line, but the new multi-cylinder Cadillac line left some observers wondering why Cadillac would build a new ultra-luxury car when average sales of its predecessor were only about 50 cars per year after the first two years. Cadillac had grown more fiscally prudent with the promotion of factory manager Nicholas Dreystadt to Cadillac general manager in 1934, so it was surprising that he would have okayed the creation of the low-volume super cars.

FINAL
ASSEMBLY LINE
›› Radiator grille, and
front and rear bumper
assembly.

MILLION
CARS

Cadillac

The last point of assembly for 1955 Cadillacs fitted each car with a bullet-crowned front bumper, grille, and rear bumper. A Series 60 Special and coupe can be seen entering this final stage of assembly. (Cadillac Historical Collection)

Few could find fault with the new V-16's beautiful exterior styling and the shock value of the car, but gone was the artfully fashioned, Owen Nacker-designed, overhead-valve power plant adorned in enamel paints and polished-aluminum parts. In its place was a more efficient flathead engine ducking between pontoon fenders. Only 514 second-generation V-16s were produced between 1938 and 1940.

During this time, Cadillac began turning its attention towards war production, supplying Allison V-1710 aircraft engine parts in 1939. By February 4, 1942, only two months after the December 7, 1941, Japanese attack on Pearl Harbor, all domestic automobile production halted.

Cadillac's contribution to the war effort included tank production. Thousands of Cadillac V-8-powered M5, M5A1, and M24 Chaffee tanks rolled out of the line at Cadillac's Clark Street plant in Detroit, and all were powered by Hydra-Matic transmissions.

The tank production not only benefited the war effort, it allowed Cadillac engineers to improve the Hydra-Matic transmission, which had only been offered in Cadillac passenger cars since 1941. Cadillac's work proficiency in war production earned it the Army-Navy "E" award for excellence, and Cadillac proudly waved the "E" flag over its Clark Street plant through the end of the war.

After the war, Cadillac went straight back to production of the pontoon-fendered models, which bore few changes from their restyled 1942 predecessors. But the gears were turning in the minds of Cadillac designers, who began drawing futuristic cars that borrowed from the war birds of World War II. Their inspiration drew heavily from Lockheed's P-38 Lightning fighter plane, a cutting-edge plane with twin booms that Harley Earl had arranged his designers to sneak a peek at before the start of American hostilities. While bubble canopies and plane nose passenger compartments were prevalent themes in early postwar Cadillac designs, it was the P-38's twin booms that made it to the final product, and tailfins were born.

Even without the fins, the fresh styling of the 1948 Cadillacs was truly revolutionary. The front fenders were swallowed into the hull and the rear fenders were on an obvious path to finding themselves integrated into the body in much the same way. A flatter and lower hood, together with the dip and rise of the rear fins, made for a more horizontal, longer, and lower look.

An enthusiastic acceptance quickly followed the car's arrival. The following year, an all-new engine of overhead-valve design was slipped between the fenders of every Cadillac sold. Lighter, more efficient, and more powerful than any flathead V-8 engine offered by Cadillac before, the 90-degree, overhead-valve engine became the blueprint for many engines to follow and is considered the forefather to the wildly successful small-block Chevrolet power plant still enjoyed by car collectors, restorers, and hot rodders. More importantly, it firmly established Cadillac as king of the luxury automobiles and a leader in performance, innovation, and technology.

The list of men behind the breakthrough Cadillac V-8 reads like a "who's who" of General Motors players. Harry F. Barr was the staff engineer in charge of Cadillac's engine design; he eventually became General Motors' engineering vice president. At the start of the engine's development in the late 1930s, Edward Cole was Cadillac's chief engineer; he rose to the presidency of General Motors. Rounding out the list of major figures was John "Jack" Gordon, who was then Cadillac's general manager; he, too, rose to the presidency of General Motors.

The influence of western movies and television was evident in the desert-fashioned showroom where this 1956 Eldorado Biarritz was displayed. (GM Media Archives)

Cadillac's typical Fleetwood Sixty Special customer enjoyed the formalness of his car in business endeavors and appreciated the sporty flair of hardtop styling, available for the first time in the Fleetwood Sixty Special in 1957. (GM Media Archives)

Famed racing sportsman Briggs Cunningham immediately put the new engine through its paces at the 1950 24 Hours of LeMans with a pair of Cadillac-based race cars. The first, a relatively stock Series 61 coupe, placed a respectable 10th overall in the race; and Cunningham's second entry, built with a more aerodynamic body and several race modifications, placed 11th overall, just behind the stock Series 61 coupe! Thanks to Cunningham, the engine had been proven beyond the highway; it was now proven on the track.

In the early 1950s, Cadillac was again involved in a war effort, helping to build tanks for the Korean Conflict. This time, however, the M-41 Walker Bulldog tanks were not Cadillac-powered, but rather they found motivation from Lycoming or Continental engines.

The war did not end automobile production, but it did affect the availability of some manufacturing supplies for automakers, including chromium materials. But once the supplies constraints were lifted, the industry was ready for the start of the chrome revolution. Flashy colors and abundant amounts of chrome made automobiles four-wheeled festivals, much to the delight of American car buyers.

A total of 146,841 new Cadillacs rolled out of the Clark Street plant in 1957 as James M. Roche took over the role of Cadillac general manager. (GM Media Archives)

Cadillac met the decade with tasteful restraint when it came to chrome, choosing to use the material to highlight the contours of the highly styled sheet metal.

A minor setback to Cadillac production came in 1953 when fire overwhelmed GM's Hydra-Matic transmission plant in Livonia, Michigan. With a shortage of transmissions, late-1953 Cadillacs were fitted with Buick's trustworthy Dynaflow transmission until Hydra-Matic production could resume.

Taking advantage of the potential built into the overhead-valve engine, Cadillac began increasing horsepower through higher compression ratios and larger carburetors. Multi-carbureted engines, standard in the sporty and luxurious Eldorados and optional in all other models beginning in 1955, saw the biggest jumps in horsepower ratings through the decade. The pony count went from 230 horsepower in the 1954 models to 270 horsepower in dual-four-barrel-equipped Cadillacs, and would continue to climb into the next decade with larger engine displacements.

On the outside, round lines from the early and mid-1950s gave way to sharp shapes as the rocket age began to influence art and design. Cadillac's styling philosophies collided with the space age by 1958, resulting in Harley Earl's retirement from the styling studios. Appreciated for their glamorous chrome and broad body features today, the 1958 Cadillacs and their corporate stable mates were initially met with disapproval for their heavy looks and overuse of chrome. A shakeup in the styling studios ousted Earl and his round, chrome-laden automobiles and paved the way for William L. Mitchell, Charles M. "Chuck" Jordan, and Dave Holls with their leaner, sharper, and lower designs.

The threesome saw Chrysler's upcoming 1957 models and they knew to compete, they would have to tone up their own cars. The first Cadillacs to react to the Chrysler competition were the wild '59s with their sky-high fins, bullet taillights, and low looks. The subsequent 1960 Cadillacs would be much cleaner—a theme which would carry Cadillac into the 1960s and beyond.

Tumultuous times marked the 1960s with the assassinations of President John F. Kennedy, his brother, Robert Kennedy, and civil rights leader

The sedans were not exempt from receiving the world's tallest production fins, which stretched from the back of every production 1959 Cadillac, including this six-window Sedan deVille. (GM Media Archives)

Cadillac had an impressive lineup of four-door models in 1962. The top-of-the-line Series 75 limousine model is the only body style left out of this photo of deVille and Series 62 four- and six-window sedans. (GM Media Archives)

Martin Luther King Jr. Civil uprisings and political polarity over the Vietnam War further shook up the American public, and Cadillac met the challenges of the volatile decade by providing stability and comfort to its clients. Fifties flash was replaced by majestic machines that showed restraint, and through the use of conveniences found nowhere else, Cadillac tried to offer its drivers an oasis from newspaper headlines.

Joining the Autronic Eye headlight dimmer on the 1964 option list were the convenient Comfort Control automatic temperature control system and the Twilight Sentinel automatic headlight. Later, electric front seat warmers and tilt-and-telescoping steering wheels would add to the Cadillac luxury experience.

But the technology built into each Cadillac went beyond the fine fabrics and luxurious leathers. Behind the classic grilles and slab-sided styling of every 1960s Cadillac burned a powerful furnace of performance. Rising engine displacements offered more powerful engines that also operated more efficiently, and by the

The restyled Fleetwoods, deVilles, and Calais reflected the safety concerns of the times and received energy-absorbing steering wheels, padded instrument panel surfaces, and a breakaway rearview mirror. Such safety concerns eventually affected sales of open models, like Alan W. Clark's 1967 deVille convertible.

A regal 1970 Cadillac Fleetwood 75 rolls down the assembly line amongst its shorter siblings at the Clark Street plant. (GM Media Archives)

end of the decade, Cadillac was featuring 472-cid engines that offered 375 horsepower. The power was needed to drive the 4,500-lb.-plus deVille and Calais models and maintain a pleasant performance level, and when installed in the front-wheel-drive Eldorado personal luxury coupes, Cadillac had a muscle car on its hands. By 1970, the Eldorado would cross the 500-cubic-inch mark with a 501-cid V-8 (often referred to as a 500), the world's largest passenger car engine. The engine would wedge its way into the Eldorado under the watch of George R. Elges, who took over the helm of Calvin J. Werner as Cadillac's general manager.

Elges presided over a period of Cadillac history when big was best. Big engines, big cars, and roomy interiors were exactly what customers wanted, and it's exactly what they received from a Cadillac. And they received them in record numbers. Cadillac crossed the 300,000-car mark for the 1973 model year, but forces beyond the control of any automobile company manager were about to make things difficult.

A short-lived 1973 embargo by oil-producing Arab nations temporarily affected the oil flow to United States shores, and stunted Cadillac and other large car sales in 1974. The market bounced back as oil supplies increased by the end of the year, but there was a lesson to be learned: Cadillacs, and all GM cars, would have to become more energy efficient. But first, Cadillac celebrated the return of oil flow by continuing to offer large engines in its larger cars, even putting the 501-cid V-8 from the Eldorado in the 1975 and 1976 full-size deVille, Calais, Fleetwood Broughams, and Series Seventy-Five sedans under the supervision of general manager Robert D. Lund, who succeeded Elges at the beginning of 1973. The only model not to receive the massive power plant was Cadillac's Euro-luxury car beater, the new 1975 Seville.

Looking to the future, Cadillac knew it had to compete with the smaller European luxury sedans from Mercedes and Jaguar, and a smaller car would also help sales in the event of another oil shortage. The Seville was that magic solution, offering mid-size dimensions and a smaller 350-cid engine. Its square lines were unusual for a Cadillac, but its level of luxury wasn't.

The remainder of the Cadillac lineup followed the Seville in a massive billion-dollar downsizing program within General Motors. All of the company's 1977 full-size cars, from the Chevrolet Impala to the Cadillac deVille, came out with smaller exterior dimensions and equal, or even larger, interior spaces than their larger 1976 counterparts. Powering the lighter full-size Cadillacs was a smaller, but still impressive, 425-cid V-8, and thanks to lighter materials and computer technology, there was less car to power. Loyal Cadillac drivers didn't miss the extra sheet metal, and the General Motors division experienced a record year with 358,487 Cadillacs rolling out the factory doors.

Cadillac's forecasting was right on the money. In 1979, Iran cut off its supply of oil to the United States, and gas stations were the scenes of long lines. Under the direction of General Manager Edward C. Kennard, Cadillac was well prepared with more fuel-efficient wedge-shaped styling on its 1980 models. For added fuel economy, Cadillac offered a staggering number of engines choices, including a V-6. It was the first time Cadillac had offered an engine with fewer than eight cylinders since 1914.

Ready for a luau, this restyled 1971 Fleetwood Eldorado convertible is surrounded by a lush Hawaiian-themed setting at an auto show. (GM Media Archives)

The most popular luxury car in the world in 1972 was the Cadillac Sedan deVille four-door hardtop. Cadillac built 99,531 of these cars for the model year. (GM Media Archives)

Cadillac honored tradition when it posed the new 1989 Coupe deVille beside the original 1949 Coupe deVille. (GM Media Archives)

The cylinder count was further decreased with the introduction of the Cimarron in late 1981. Careful not to label the subcompact a Cadillac, advertising touted the Cavalier-based sedan as "Cimarron, by Cadillac." Many felt the 1.8-liter, four-cylinder car tarnished the Cadillac image and offered little for the large price difference over a J-car Pontiac Sunbird or Chevrolet Cavalier. As a result, sales for the Cimarron remained disappointing throughout its days on Cadillac lots.

With the adoption of front-wheel drive, the thoroughly redesigned 1985 deVille and Fleetwood models received a far better welcome from Cadillac buyers. Smaller and lighter, the new generation of Cadillacs was more prepared to battle the encroaching luxury cars from BMW, Mercedes-Benz, and Lincoln. Seville and Eldorado also benefited from European-influenced styling the following year with decreased amounts of chrome, composite headlamps, and smoother lines.

Realizing a centerpiece was needed to add luster to the Cadillac nameplate, the company worked with Sergio Pininfarina to build the sporty, two-seat Allanté, which hit showrooms for the 1987 model year. Pininfarina reportedly said working with Cadillac on the Allanté project was "the realization of a lifelong dream." With its 4.1-liter V-8 tweaked for performance, the Italian-built convertible succeeded in injecting a youthful spirit into Cadillac's image.

Allanté's mission was to attract new customers, but Cadillac also took steps to please the customers it already had. Longtime Cadillac customers complained that the 1985 deVilles and front-wheel-drive Fleetwoods lacked the length Cadillacs were known for, and the company took steps to cleverly lengthen the models through taillight extensions and a handsome, restyled grille and headlight arrangement. The revision would carry Cadillac proudly until the completely redesigned 1994 models debuted.

In the meantime, Cadillac attacked the import luxury market with all-new Seville and Eldorado models in 1992. Smooth, clean surfaces and a minimum of bright work, combined with the powerful 4.9-liter engine, made the luxury coupe and sedan competitors on all fronts. The pair was the first product of a 1987 reorganization that made Cadillac the only General Motors division with control over its own engineering, manufacturing, marketing, and sales activities. The reorganization put general manager John O. Grettenberger in charge of engineering and manufacturing, while Robert L. Dorn provided leadership as the director of operations for the division.

Cadillac started building cars with utility in mind and later moved into luxury. With the introduction of the 1999 Escalade and 2002 EXT (above), Cadillac matched luxury with utility. (GM Media Archives)

Cadillac brought in the new millennium with an all-new 2000 DeVille sedan. The car was slightly shorter and narrower than the car it replaced, but the wheelbase was lengthened for added ride comfort in an overall sporty package. (GM Media Archives)

By 1994, Cadillac's entire lineup had been constructed from cocktail napkin to rolling machine under Cadillac's autonomous framework. Even the Fleetwood Brougham, which had gone largely unchanged since its last major redesign in 1980, was completely new. There was also an addition to the lineup: a small, youth market-fetching sedan touting perky V-6 power, a smaller body than other Cadillacs, and a smaller price tag. Christened the "Catera," the sporty, Opel-based sedan found it difficult to escape comparison to the Cavalier-based Cimarron even before its late-1996 introduction, and sales were modest. By 2002, the Catera was gone.

But Cadillac wasn't ready to abandon the market targeted by the Catera. Instead, the midsize sedan served as a warning to the competition that Cadillac would be launching a full-scale attack on the market segment occupied by

The fabulous Cadillac XLR.

sporty BMW and Mercedes-Benz models. The weapon was the all-new CTS, a knife-edged sport sedan with uncompromising performance and cutting-edge style.

The sharp lines of the CTS were the result of a common goal between GM Design Chief Wayne K. Cherry and Cadillac General Manager John F. Smith. As far back as 1997, the pair aimed to meld Cadillac's advanced technology with stunning looks. The plan was named "Art & Science," and its mission was to reestablish Cadillac's leadership role in the entire automobile industry.

Success has followed the CTS in its brief life on the market. Cadillac has attracted new buyers who are finding that the CTS is more than just good looks and a concentration of Cadillac technology; it is a driver's car that begs to be pushed through the corners and wound through back-road straightaways.

The CTS is just the beginning of big plans for Cadillac in the luxury car marketplace. The sporty XLR two-seat retractable roadster, hitting dealers in late 2003, promises the same thrilling driving experience with the added punch of V-8 power. Current Cadillac General Manager Mark LaNeve has promised that the CTS will also benefit from two more cylinders of power with the upcoming V-8-powered V-Series.

Art & Science reform has even reached Cadillac's family-hauling Escalade, EXT, ESV, and the new SRX models, which all share the razor edges of the CTS and XLR.

The world is keeping a watchful on Cadillac's styling renaissance, but it's likely few are following Cadillac more closely than Robert A. Lutz, General Motors' vice chairman of product development and chairman of GM North America. Lutz joined General Motors after revitalizing Chrysler's products in the 1990s with exciting cars like the Dodge Viper and Plymouth Prowler.

Lutz's arrival postdates Cadillac's Art & Science movement, and his eye for design has already touched the upcoming STS models, which are expected to carry softer, more sweeping lines at Lutz's request.

Showing a preference for less aggressive lines, Lutz believes that softer, more luxurious lines are more befitting of the Cadillac crest, but he has stated that he's willing to change them. If the CTS's early success is an accurate measurement of the edgy styling's acceptance, Cadillac has already begun slicing into the competition and proven it is worthy of its leadership position.

Culture

The pride of presidents. The chariot of celebrities.
The wheels of the wealthy. Cadillac is the
inspiration and aspiration of drivers around the
world. The dream of Cadillac ownership oozes
through the American psyche, surfacing through
songs, movies, and even the lifestyles of respected
figures. So entrenched in the American lifestyle is
the word "Cadillac" that it has become a synonym
for success and superiority.

Cadillac's image was largely established through
advertising, which first spoke of Cadillac quality
and dependability. Early ads declaring "the power of
a Cadillac never diminishes," and "it's just good all
over" helped the public put trust in the marque's
character.

100 Years

Finding comfort worthy of a queen in an early Cadillac was silent movie actress Ann May, who had a very special Cadillac built by Don Lee, the West Coast's largest Cadillac distributor. Another notable name in Cadillac history, Harley Earl, designed the Victoria-style touring car for Miss May. The unique styling of May's dual-windshield, open-front touring car would have surely stood tall among the other Cadillacs and Packards on a Hollywood set, which likely drew additional clients to Lee's shop and the Cadillac chassis. Numerous other celebrities living around Lee's Hollywood shop are known to have entrusted the styling pen of Earl to create personalized bodies on their Cadillac chassis before the designer was lured over to General Motors.

By the 1920s, Cadillac was posing its automobiles before pillared mansions and landscaped driveways to reflect the class and elegance built into its automobiles. Swooning over the stylish ads, societal nobles began piloting their own Cadillacs and LaSalles, which even furthered the Cadillac image. The romance sketched into the black-and-white pencil and pen-and-ink drawings is known to have mesmerized Hollywood screen stars Clara Bow into a 1927 LaSalle roadster and Delores Del Rio into a 1928 Cadillac seven-passenger sedan.

What better way to get Junior to the football game than in a 1918 Cadillac Type 57 tourer? The V-8 under the hood of Mom's Cadillac received detachable cylinder heads and an improved transmission that year. (GM Media Archives)

Truly a chariot for royalty, this 1930 Pinin Farina-built boattail speedster was ordered by the Maharajah of Orccha and was built with provisions for the rear-seated Maharajah to hunt tigers in his domain, the province of Bhopal, India. The one-of-a-kind, right-hand-drive V-16 has the unique distinction of marking the beginning of a styling relationship between Cadillac and Pinin Farina. (Blackhawk Classic Auto Collection photo; Old Cars Weekly archives)

The confident and elegant styling of Cadillacs attracted a growing Hollywood clientele through the 1920s, but the introduction of the V-16 and V-12 models made Cadillac a star. Such cars were not cheap, but it was worth pulling up to the red carpet on opening night seated in a Cadillac badged with the menacing V-16 or V-12 emblem shining in the barrage of camera flashes.

The silent meets the sonorous: this 1931 Cadillac Fleetwood town car, powered by the famously quiet V-16 engine, was owned by Madame Ernestine Schumann-heink, the famous Metropolitan Opera contralto. (Old Cars Weekly archives)

Cadillacs continue to be the stars of any gathering of people and automobiles, but a one-of-a-kind Cadillac like this Lancefield of London-bodied 1931 Cadillac V-16 even stands out above its peers. The right-hand-drive, three-position Victoria sports unusual bucket seats and aluminum wheel discs and is a rare example of a V-16 chassis without semi-custom Fleetwood bodywork. (Gregg D. Merksamer photo)

General Motors brought the automobile to the masses in many ways. Big city auto shows and GM's own Motorama and GM Parade of Progress were just some of the methods the company reached out beyond advertising to create excitement for its products. This 1936 Parade of Progress caravan is being led by a 1936 Cadillac convertible sedan. (GM Media Archives)

Hollywood sex symbol Mae West found elegance worthy of her stature in this Fleetwood-bodied 1934 Cadillac V-12 town car. (Old Cars Weekly archives)

A V-16 Cadillac would rob any couple of the spotlight on their important day, especially a Series 452 V-16 as rare as this All-Weather Sport Phaeton. (Angelo Van Bogart collection)

Royalty and celebrities gravitated to the Cadillac crest, sometimes with special requests. Cadillac was happy to oblige, as was the case when the Duke of Windsor wanted a custom 1941 Cadillac. This lithe sedan, which the Duke named "Dutchess," features the flow-through styling usually found on Buicks of the 1940s. (GM Media Archives)

image to enhance their own, but it was a give-and-take relationship. The Broadway play "Madam X" loaned its name to a special series of elegant closed V-16 body styles after Harley Earl had dinner with Pauline Fredericks, the play's star. The lofty price tag of the Madam X cars would, coincidentally, limit purchasers to successful actors and actresses, and wealthy businessmen.

The Depression was a wonderful time to live the American dream, if one was wealthy. Moneyed luminaries living the Cadillac lifestyle after the 1929 Wall Street crash were few, but Cadillac sold an amazing 2,887 1930 V-16's in a large cast of Fleetwood-built body designs during the 1930 model year. Well-known band leader Paul Whiteman, film producer Cecil B. De Mille, and screen legend Constance Bennett were among the many stars who indulged in a V-16 Cadillac.

For the discreet customer, Cadillac offered a wide variety of dignified and reserved formal bodies on its chassis. These seven-passenger sedans and limousines were largely the choice of respectable businessmen and social dignitaries, but underworld characters also found that understated, silent, and smooth sedans allowed them to slither between speakeasies. When endowed with the powerful V-16 and V-12 engines, the stealthy sedans made for excellent get-away cars.

The Cadillac's potential wasn't lost on Chicago-area gangster Al Capone, who

After entertaining thousands of soldiers during World War II, Bob Hope was rewarded with a new 1946 Cadillac. (Cadillac Historical Collection)

Bing Crosby sang himself into a spot behind the wheel of a sporty 1947 Cadillac convertible. (Cadillac Historical Collection)

The handsome Fleetwood Sixty Special of 1949 gets fawned over at the New York Auto Show. (GM Media Archives)

Most Americans saw Cadillac's new jewel, the Eldorado, for the first time when President Dwight D. Eisenhower waved to his constituents from the backseat of the new luxury car in his inaugural parade in January, 1953. (Cadillac Historical Collection)

The glitz and glamour of the neon-glowing streets of 1950s Las Vegas, Nevada, was matched by the vibrant colors and gleaming chrome of a new Cadillac.

Roy Rogers made his tin horse a 1947 Cadillac. Whether they were country boys or city boys, the Hollywood set made Cadillac their choice of transportation. (Cadillac Historical Collection)

was known to creep around in the cloak of night in his armor-plated 1930 Cadillac V-16 sedan. The presence of the mighty engine also ensured Capone could careen around Chicago streets when the need arose, and other Cadillacs joined his stable. Gangster Ma Barker also enjoyed Cadillac luxury and power, though from a later V-12 sedan.

Criminal admirers did little to tarnish Cadillac's reputation during the poverty-stricken 1930s. Through the magic of movies and the media, a bond between successful people and their automobiles was being pounded into the minds of moviegoers. On rare occasions when an afternoon flick at the local movie house could be afforded, ticket buyers could watch their favorite stars perform from behind the wheel of luxury cars they could only dream of owning, and in some cases, even seeing.

Producers of "The Carpetbaggers" placed actor Alan Ladd in a V-16 dual-cowl

The Solid Gold Cadillac was the first major motion picture to include the name of America's favorite luxury car in its title. The 1956 film starred Judy Holliday, Paul Douglas, and the pictured gold 1956 Cadillac Eldorado Biarritz convertible; other Cadillacs made guest appearances throughout the movie as well.

Cadillac quality and performance were tested on many paved surfaces, but the same attributes that made Cadillacs winners on the streets also made them popular at county fair demolition derbies across the country once their domestic life was finished. Here, a 1954 Cadillac Fleetwood Sixty Special and a 1956 Coupe deVille battle it out gladiator style.

This couple admires the fine lines of the freshly restyled 1954 Cadillac. (Cadillac Historical Collection)

phaeton, outfitted with Hollywood bullhorns and cowhide upholstery. In 1935, actor Robert Taylor lit up the screen with a 1933 Cadillac that had an integral part in the plot of "Magnificent Obsession." Off the screen, stars continued to choose Cadillac and helped the company move a significant amount of V-16s and V-12s off their lots. Joan Crawford was escorted in a 1933 V-16 town car. Marlene Dietrich was a conisseur of fine cars and owner of a 1935 V-16 town car and 1933 V-16 town car similar to Crawford's. Duke Ellington enjoyed open-air motoring in a V-16 roadster. Al Jolson was the owner of a 1933 V-16 all-weather phaeton. And Jean Harlow traveled in a 1934 V-12 town car.

Although V-12 and V-16 ownership was afforded by few, Cadillac advertisement appealed to the masses through The Depression by tempting magazine subscribers with attractively priced LaSalles and V-8 Cadillacs. Artwork still reflected the pleasures of Cadillac ownership and built upon the prestigious elements of driving a Cadillac, but the company wasn't afraid to recite its prices for entry-level coupes and roadsters. That would all change when America was thrust into World War II. With its focus radically altered, Cadillac declared its role in tank building and aircraft engine parts manufacturing. A 1945 ad trumpeted that the U.S. war effort had "the imprint of Cadillac power."

With automobile production ceased through the war, drivers were forced to

Elegance. Style. Grace. A sporty 1954 Cadillac Eldorado carried all of these characteristics, making it a worthy chariot for a woman of equal form. (GM Media Archives)

Elvis Presley rocked his way into homes and hearts across the world with his music and movies. One of his first rewards was a new Cadillac. Several other Cadillacs followed, including this Fleetwood Sixty Special added to his collection early in his career. Presley had the Cadillac repainted pink before taking delivery and eventually gave it to his mother. Said to be his favorite car, the Fleetwood Sixty Special was never sold or given away like many of the other Cadillacs and other luxury cars Presley owned. It still remains at The King's Graceland home. (Elvis image used by permission, Elvis Presley Enterprises, Inc.©)

Perhaps the moment that inspired "Jailhouse Rock": Elvis is shown getting stopped by a man of the law in his 1956 Eldorado Biarritz. Elvis purportedly walked into a paint shop, smashed grapes on the front fender of this Cadillac, and requested that it be painted in a similar purple color. (Elvis image used by permission, Elvis Presley Enterprises, Inc.©)

Virginia Ruth Egnor was a busty blond who went by the name Dagmar on NBC's 1950s late-night talk show "Broadway Open House." During the same time period, Cadillacs began sprouting a pair of protrusions from their front bumpers, and since the cars had long been connected to celebrities, the comparison of the bumper feature and Dagmar's chest was perfect. This 1957 Cadillac struts its "Dagmars" alongside an unnamed model. (GM Media Archives)

This leading lady exudes the class that Cadillac depicted in much of the advertising used to sell its cars through the 1950s: white gloves, high heels, and a stylish dress. (Cadillac Historical Collection)

stretch the lives of their automobiles, and durability became the test of a car make's value. Cadillac's precision manufacturing and quality workmanship withstood the test, and coming out of the war, the company was able to report, in a 1945 advertisement headlined with "I know what I'll buy first," that more Cadillac owners than any other marque "intended to 'repeat' on their present cars."

The real-world tests of the war years did more for the marque's reputation than any movie or star ever could, and Cadillac was backlogged with orders for new cars once assembly lines stopped pumping out tanks and resumed automobile production. But that didn't stop Cadillac from using celebrity purchases to enhance its reputation. When western film star Roy Rogers took delivery of his 1947 Cadillac, photographers were on hand to shoot the event. Comedian Bob Hope, who had entertained thousands of homesick World War II American GI's, also examined a new Cadillac before cameras.

With patriotism running strong following the war, Cadillac's design move to imitate the tail appendages on the famous P-38 fighter planes used to win the war scored big with buyers. The new fins borrowed from the P-38 and employed on the 1948 Cadillacs reminded Americans of Cadillac's successful contributions to the war effort, yet added that touch of flamboyance found in the prestigious classic-era Cadillacs. Cadillac's next golden age was about to begin.

The combination of cutting-edge technology of the overhead-valve V-8 of 1949

A model beholds the beauty of a shark-finned 1957 Cadillac Eldorado that was as fashionable as the model herself. (GM Media Archives)

The ultimate expression of 1950s flash and flamboyance is depicted in the wild 1959 Cadillacs. It just doesn't get any wilder than Rick Case's bright red 1959 Cadillac Eldorado Biarritz convertible with its rocket ship rear end and flashy front grille work.

with the fins of 1948 made Cadillac a hard package to beat. Soon, Cadillac was reliving its glory on the screen and in the garages of the rich and famous. With television coming into the homes of Americans, celebrities had yet another creative outlet to display their lifestyle, which often included a Cadillac in the garage. Firmly ahead of luxury competitors Lincoln and Packard in sales, Cadillac became the ultimate success symbol. Owning a Cadillac was the ultimate way to declare "I have arrived."

No cultural icon brought more to Cadillac's image in the 1950s than hip-swinging rock 'n' roller Elvis Presley. The musician and movie star elevated himself out of poverty and into fame and fortune, and one of his first rewards was a Cadillac. Presley's most famous Cadillac was his pink 1955 Fleetwood sedan that had originally been painted gray by the factory, but Presley immediately had it repainted pink and eventually gifted the car to his mother, Gladys, whom he loved dearly. Presley kept the car after her 1958 death, and it remains on display at his Graceland estate as a symbol of his success.

With the simple color change, Presley transformed his understated 1955 Fleetwood into an emblem of the youthful energy in America's prosperous postwar years. Like Presley's career and his Fleetwood, Cadillac's own products would grow increasingly wild with vibrant bends of sheet metal and growing physical stature. Like Presley himself, Cadillacs were larger than life, and Americans wanted a piece of the dream.

Exciting times called for exciting cars, and Cadillac delivered with finned and chrome-laden machines. One didn't need rock 'n' roll in his blood to appreciate the excitement and symbolism of a Cadillac, and the marque was rewarded with record-breaking sales through the 1950s and into the 1960s. Celebrities continued to be enamored with the luxury marque's products, and Cadillac gained additional publicity through film and television as a result.

Often the co-star but never the star, Cadillac earned a spot in the title and a co-starring role in 1956's *The Solid Gold Cadillac*. The comedy about corporate corruption starred Judy Holliday and Paul Douglas and featured a gold-gilded yellow 1956 Eldorado Biarritz convertible, for which the movie was named. Hundreds of movies have since been named after America's favorite luxury car.

Crooner Frank Sinatra was more typical of Cadillac's elite clientele in the '50s. In his pressed suit and satin shoes, Sinatra dripped with the elegant lifestyle. Sinatra owned many fine cars throughout his lifetime, but the one best fitting his martini-mixing lifestyle was, perhaps, his Eldorado Brougham. The ultra-expensive Brougham was Cadillac's top offering and featured many striking

Glowing like "Christine" from the Stephen King novel, this stunning 1959 Cadillac Series 62 convertible awaits its master and his damsel outside the Detroit Institute of Art. (GM Media Archives)

Rat Pack member Sammy Davis, Jr. looks over some paperwork on the hood of a new 1956 Eldorado. (Cadillac Historical Collection)

Even today, probably nothing typifies the 1950s more than the 1959 Cadillac Series 62 convertible. The car has graced everything from stamps to napkins to greeting cards.

General Motors, Chrysler Corporation, and Ford Motor Company each provided special limousine versions of their grandest automobiles for Queen Elizabeth II's Royal Tour of the United States and Canada. Cadillac's Series 75 limousine was selected from General Motors' lineup and fitted with a clear plastic cover over the rear passenger compartment, shown here protecting President John F. Kennedy and First Lady Jacqueline Kennedy, much like the landaulet-style limousines of the Classic era. (Cadillac Historical Collection)

Just because the 1960 Cadillacs were toned down doesn't mean they lost their wild styling touches, exemplified in this glamorous photo of a Marilyn Monroe look-alike and her accessorizing poodle. (GM Media Archives)

Cadillac never forgot the romance of a convertible and tempted the senses with this dramatic shot of the skeg-carrying 1961 Cadillac Series 62 convertible and young couple. (GM Media Archives)

features, including a stainless-steel roof, mouton carpeting, an unusually low profile, and the ultimate set of accessories for a night on the town. Included in the set were a plastic cigarette case, a beveled mirror, six metallic tumblers, an Evans compact, and an ArpËge perfume atomizer, among other personal items. Sinatra's Brougham is believed to be the car used in the ultimate Rat Pack movie, "Ocean's Eleven." Wrapped in an ermine stole, honorary Rat Packer Shirley McLaine stumbles out of the Nairobi Pearl Brougham and into the arms of fellow Pack member Dean Martin in one scene.

Other screen and performing legends also enjoyed the decadent pleasures of Cadillac ownership. Hollywood actress Jayne Mansfield felt the southern California air flow through her blond hair from behind the wheel of a 1959 Cadillac Eldorado Biarritz convertible. As if the flamboyance of the rocket taillights and skyward-pointing fins weren't enough, Mansfield's Eldorado was painted in an equally ostentatious bright pink—her favorite color.

With the disappearance of competing luxury brands in The Depression years of the 1930s, Cadillac came to dominate the parking lots of movie premiers and the Hollywood set by the 1950s. Award galas became perfect places to spot Cadillacs. In a throwback to the custom coach-building companies of the past, some stars had their Cadillacs personalized to stand out from their peers.

Pianist Liberace was one such Cadillac owner. To set his 1954 Cadillac Eldorado apart, Liberace had California car customizer George Barris trim the seats in his Eldorado's interior with a grand piano pattern, complete with keys and his trademark candelabra. Dancing notes covered the bottom portion of both the front and back seat for a look as unique as the car's owner.

Leadership for leaders

Cadillac's image as an automobile of power was boosted early by President Woodrow Wilson. The American leader was shuttled to Boston for a World War I victory parade in a 1919 touring car, making him the first president of many to enjoy the service of a Cadillac. Wilson's choice of chariots was appropriate because many other Cadillac touring cars and limousines had served on the battlefield during the conflict in Europe.

Cadillac hit the newsreels when a pair of Fleetwood-built 1938 V-16 convertible sedans were added to the president's motorcade. Each sedan used the new flathead V-16 engine on a unique, monstrous, 165-inch wheelbase and came equipped with sirens and handles for Secret Service agents. The cars were used well into the 1960s and can be seen in footage of presidents from Franklin D. Roosevelt to John F. Kennedy.

Cadillacs continued to have serious roles in the 1950s and 1960s, too. A second pair of stretched Cadillac convertible sedans were delivered to the White House in 1956 for the employ of America's commander in chief. Coachbuilder Hess & Eisenhardt constructed the pair of open 1956 Cadillacs, dubbed the "Queen Mary II" and "Queen Elizabeth II," and included running boards, rear steps, and a siren, among other special equipment to aid its primary passengers, usually

Cadillacs have been immortalized in many different mediums from music to art, but the most unusual ode to America's favorite luxury marque is Cadillac Ranch. The popular tourist site was built by a millionaire in 1974 in a wheat field outside of Amarillo, Texas. It receives thousands of visitors a year, as evidenced by the layers of graffiti covering the lineup of finned Cadillacs. (Jerry Heasley photo)

Nearly each generation of fin is represented at Cadillac Ranch, from a second-year 1949 Sedanette to a 1963 sedan. Cadillac Ranch is appropriately placed near Route 66, the famed east-west link to California. (Jerry Heasley photo)

Secret Service agents. The cars were used well into the 1970s, and one of them is best known for being the back-up car behind the Lincoln carrying President John F. Kennedy on the day of his assassination in Dallas, Texas.

Kennedy, and his wife Jacqueline, had other Cadillacs at their disposal. Cadillac, along with Chrysler and Ford, built limousines for Queen Elizabeth II's Royal Tour through Canada and the United States. The queen and the first lady were widely photographed in a 1959 Fleetwood Series 75 with the rear portion of its roof cut out like a 1930s landaulet model. In the absent sheet metal's place was a detachable clear plastic covering for the portion behind the rear door and into the roof. The president was also photographed entering a 1962 Cadillac Fleetwood sedan in the 1960s.

While the country was experiencing growing political turmoil, the flash and luxury of the finned 1964 Cadillacs provided an oasis of comfort, an idea not lost on this fur-toting femme posed before the exclusive 1964 Fleetwood Eldorado. Note this car's non-production wheels. (GM Media Archives)

Looking as though it would fit into Hawaii's Hana Highway, this 1970 Cadillac coupe at the plant-filled Chicago Auto Show is ready to eat a slice of highway with its windows down. (GM Media Archives)

The politically turbulent 1960s meant changes in the way prominent figures were chauffeured around, and limousines with open construction were all but eliminated for safety reasons. Cadillac's next presidential limousine, an armor-plated 1984 Fleetwood with bullet-proof glass windows and a taller roof for added visibility to the president, was delivered to President Ronald Reagan. A second car, a landaulet-style 1984 Fleetwood built by Hess & Eisenhardt, was used as a follow-up car and acted in the same capacity for the Secret Service as had the Queen Mary II and Queen Elizabeth II 1956 Cadillacs.

Less than 10 years later, a new Cadillac limousine was added to the presidential fleet, this one for President Bill Clinton. Unlike previous Cadillac presidential limousines, the 1993 Fleetwood Brougham was designed, developed, and manufactured completely by General Motors. Like Reagan's 1984 Fleetwood, the 1993 model featured a tall roof with similar armor-plating security measures throughout.

Cadillac's newest presidential limousine, a 2001 Cadillac DeVille, was unveiled in President George W. Bush's inaugural parade with the first use of the company's new wreath and crest emblem. But that isn't all that was new. The presidential Cadillac, considered the most technologically advanced car in the world, features state-of-the-art protection and communications systems. Hand

Cadillac made a historic corporate connection with the People's Republic of China when it sold a fleet of 20 Cadillacs, including this Fleetwood Seventy Five limousine, to the communist government in 1985.

built by GM's Special Vehicle Group, the limousine is actually longer, taller, and wider than production DeVilles, while maintaining some of the basic dimensions of a standard DeVille. This creation is the latest visible symbol of Cadillac's ever-evolving role in creating and reflecting American culture.

To the tune of culture

Cadillac culture permeated into American homes through the speakers of Zenith, Motorola, and RCA home radio consoles. Wonderbar and Delco radios glowing from the dashboards of automobiles brought Cadillac-inspired tunes to the roads across America. The Playmates' "Beep Beep" was an early ode to Cadillac performance in which a Cadillac tops out at more than 100 mph to beat a Nash Rambler coming up on its tail. In a twist with more fantasy than fact, the Rambler succeeds in overtaking the Cadillac in second gear. Country singer Johnny Cash, a Cadillac owner himself, sang the hit tune "One Piece at a Time," about the extreme lengths a fictional character will go through to fulfill his desire to own a Cadillac. In Cash's song, a factory worker builds a Cadillac from parts he snuck out in his lunchbox.

Other country stars have sang and written odes to Cadillac, including Chris LeDoux, Garth Brooks, and Dwight Yoakam, but the latest wave of celebrity endorsement comes from the rap music genre. Artists, including Ludacris, Snoop Dogg, and 50 Cent, toss lyrics about their custom-painted Cadillacs with custom wheels and decibel-testing stereo systems. Particularly popular with rap stars and athletes are Cadillac's Escalade and DeVille, both of which have found their way into many recent song lyrics. Now more than ever, the best way to say you've arrived is to breeze up in a Cadillac.

Old meets new: A Crimson Pearl 2001 Cadillac Eldorado ETC strolling on the turf of its 1959 Cadillac Eldorado Biarritz ancestor. (GM Media Archives)

Innovation

Forging the future has always been Cadillac's self-imposed task. With quality its number-one priority, Cadillac has engineered many technological firsts throughout its history and earned admiration and respect from its competitors. For some automakers, breakthroughs come on the race track and in sales numbers, but for Cadillac these achievements stemmed from technology.

Cadillac's birth and success is based on innovation, and its founder began with the heart of his new machine: its engine. By improving on the Oldsmobile engine by precision-grinding its parts and fine tuning its design, Henry Leland created what would be the single-cylinder soul of the first Cadillacs, though that was not his intention.

100 Years

The engine was actually destined for Ransom E. Olds' motor car, but when Olds realized how expensive it would be to create new toolings for the engine, he rejected Leland's triumph.

Leland didn't have to wait long for takers. When investors William Murphy and Lemuel Brown consulted Leland regarding the dissolution of the Henry Ford Company, Leland suggested they create their own automobile company with his precision-ground innovation. The three agreed and placed Leland and his son, Wilfred, in charge.

Debuted at the New York Auto Show, the investors' Cadillac was a hit and sold out. Awed by the power and efficiency put forth by the one-lunger, the public showed its confidence in Leland's revolutionary method of building engines, and clawed at the doors for more. Other manufacturers took note and eventually followed Leland's engine-building process; it would not be the last time automotive engineers looked to Cadillac for leadership. Engines manufactured by competing brands often guzzled oil and fuel and were temperamental, but not the Cadillac's. There was no sign of these problems, thanks to the use of precision gauges that made each piston exactly alike to fit perfectly into any cylinder jacket manufactured by Cadillac. Leland and his engineers scrapped many engine components and gauges in the quest for perfection. Parts for each Cadillac were tested to a miniscule 1/1000th of an inch, truly unheard of in the dawn of automobile construction.

Cadillac innovation didn't end with the fitting of parts in that inaugural year. A busy Henry Leland also integrated a cutting-edge cam-and-lever system into

To prove the strength of the Charles F. Kettering-designed DELCO self starter, Cadillac stacked 12 passengers on its four-cylinder chassis and drove them around the room, using only the power of the self-starting device for movement. (GM Media Archives)

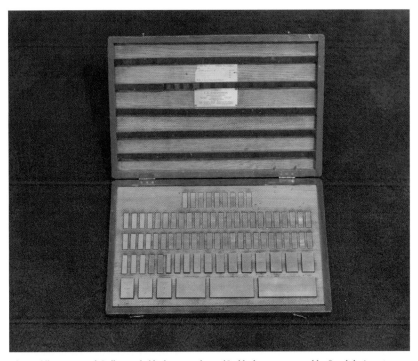

The Cadillac Historical Collection holds the original set of Jo-block gauges created by Swedish-American toolmaker Carl Edward Johansson and used by Cadillac to check its own working gauges. The tools allowed Cadillac to save time and money in the manufacture of its precision-crafted automobiles beginning around 1907. (Cadillac Historical Collection)

his automobile that allowed the driver to adjust engine speed and load via a carrying intake valve lift. Amazingly, Leland's cam-and-lever system can still be found on some luxury cars today.

Even the smallest details were not ignored. The new Cadillac also came fitted with special split-core fasteners that locked a nut on its thread, making the use of a lock washer unnecessary.

By engineering and producing his own engines, Leland was able to control the fate of the Cadillac. Competitors were not as lucky. Most pieced their car's power plant together from parts supplied by other companies, putting their quality at the mercy of the part builder.

A system of gauges dubbed "Go" and "Not Go" ensured mechanical parts destined for a Cadillac would meet strict fit and finish expectations. The system worked like this: First, a part was measured with a "Go" gauge to determine if it was large enough. If it passed, the part was then subjected to the "Not Go" gauge. If it passed, it was installed in a Cadillac. If not, and the part could be machined to fit, a Cadillac craftsman would correct it. Parts that could not be corrected were scrapped in the name of precision engineering.

Cadillac introduced the world's first mass-produced V-16 in 1930, and the smooth exterior of the beautifully designed V-16 reflected the silky operation of the hydraulic lash adjusters in the 160-horsepower, 452-cid overhead-valve engine. Ron Hickman's right-hand-drive 1930 V-16 dual-cowl phaeton makes the occasional visit to France and England. (Photo courtesy of Robert Maidment)

Al and Maurine Edmond's 1932 Cadillac 355-B five-passenger coupe, like all Cadillacs, featured silent helical gears in the Synchro-Mesh transmission in all three forward speeds, adjustable two-way hydraulic shock absorbers, free wheeling, and a vacuum-operated automatic clutch. (Angelo Van Bogart photo)

This regal Fleetwood-bodied 1933 Cadillac seven-passenger sedan owned by Malcolm Willits displays the Fisher no-draft ventilation system introduced by Cadillac and LaSalle on closed 1933 models.

Leland took standardization to the next level when he adopted the use of J-blocks, which were a creation of Swedish toolmaker Carl Edward Johansson. The partnership of Leland and Johansson was inevitable as few other manufacturers of the time could have fully appreciated Johansson's invention. In his quest for standardization of parts, Leland envisioned how the small metal measuring blocks could improve the manufacturing of his automobile, and they did. When put into use in 1907, the instruments allowed Cadillac mechanics to check the accuracy of the existing gauges that measured the parts put into each Cadillac.

The ultimate test of Leland's standardized part manufacturing came only one year later when the Royal Automobile Club disassembled three random one-cylinder Cadillacs imported by British Cadillac dealer Frederick Stanley Bennett. Club mechanics then jumbled each Cadillac's parts into a heap and reassembled the parts back into a working Cadillac. Each Cadillac was restarted, two with only a single crank and the third after two pulls, and then subjected to a 500-mile spin around the freshly carved Brooklands Metrodome track. Each member of the Cadillac triumvirate performed flawlessly and even averaged an impressive 34 mph. Cadillac earned a "Certificate of Performance" from the club. Soon after, Cadillac became the first American manufacturer to win the coveted Dewar Trophy, presented by Sir Thomas Dewar himself.

Through the genius of a young engineer, Cadillac began setting itself up for another Dewar Trophy win in 1909. The engineer, Charles Franklin Kettering, had already gained fame for his electric cash register that eliminated the need for cranking. He would soon do the same for the automobile, but before that would happen, he had to solve the need for a magneto to charge an automobile. Kettering accomplished this by developing an ignition system that combined a car's four induction coils into one unit that was not affected by vibration and was heat resistant. The system allowed a battery's power to be preserved for longer periods by ceasing rapid coil fire. The new ignition system also replaced the vibrators in the coil with one set of contact points that connected to a condenser that could pull electrical current from the points to lengthen their life.

Kettering had been testing the system on his own Cadillac roadster, and when he was pleased with the system, he wrote to Henry Leland with a description of his accomplishment, then followed up with visits to the Cadillac factory. Leland soon sent an engineer who had been with the company since the start, Ernest Sweet, to examine the system. After a day of riding around in the roadster, Sweet left impressed and shared his experience with Leland. An appreciation and trust in innovation led Leland to contract Kettering and his partner, E. A. Deeds, for 8,000 ignition systems, which would be installed on the 1910 models. After the initial panic of having to manufacture several thousand systems for a car known for its reliability and performance, the pair set to work and contracted Kellogg Switchboard and Supply Company of Chicago to build the ignition systems for their own company, dubbed the Dayton Engineering Laboratories Company, which was shortened to "DELCO." The scene was now set for an innovation that would rock the automobile industry.

Cadillac excited crowds at the 1933 Chicago Century of Progress Exposition with its Series 452C Aero-Dynamic Coupe. An all-metal top, pontoon fenders, and fastback styling was ahead of anything else on the road. Cadillac was compelled to add the Aero-Dynamic Coupe to its catalog of semi-custom bodies, and a total of 20 were built on V-8, V-12, and V-16 chassis from 1934 to 1937. The original 1933 show car, pictured here, has never been traced. (Cadillac Historical Collection)

Severe and thorough testing of the system worked out the flaws and ensured customer satisfaction, but to ease the minds of skeptical Cadillac buyers, the traditional magneto system was also included on each Cadillac sold.

Only two years later, Kettering and his fellow engineers solved the dangerous dilemma of crank-starting automobiles by developing a system that would complement their DELCO ignition. The system would forever eliminate the need to crank-start an automobile. Working with his team of Cadillac engineers, Kettering created a component that would turn the engine over enough to fire it, then allow the battery to be charged through a generator once the automobile was running. The generator was part of an entirely new lighting system and ignition system that allowed Cadillacs to run electric lamps.

Entirely new audiences could be comfortable behind the wheel or tiller of an automobile. Men and women without the strength to crank-start an automobile gained new independence as they no longer needed a chauffer. All drivers could drive confidently at night with the road solidly illuminated before them. Truly, the DELCO system was nothing short of revolutionary.

The innovation didn't get past the motoring public, Cadillac competitors, or the Royal Automobile Club. After starting the Cadillac 1,000 consecutive times without fail, the organization awarded Cadillac the Dewar Trophy a second time. No other automobile manufacturer in the world could lay claim to that honor.

1938 New York Auto Show spectators examine Cadillac's second-generation V-16 engine. The goal of Cadillac's chief engineer, Ernest W. Seaholm, in developing the L-head engine was to produce a V-16 with fewer parts, less weight, and power equal to that of its overhead-valve predecessor. Seaholm succeeded. (GM Media Archives)

Cadillac's technological achievements were earned on its legendary single- and four-cylinder engines, but even before the self-starting system was developed, Cadillac's competitors and spendier contemporaries were offering powerful six-cylinder engines that offered loads of power and torque. By the end of 1914, Cadillac was ready to "two-up" them by offering a V-shaped eight-cylinder engine with the same effortless power and smooth, quiet operation that had been a Cadillac hallmark since Leland began producing cars.

The new Cadillac V-8 thundered across the industry not because it was the first V-8 engine, but because it was the first to be mass produced. Equally important was that it was available in a mid-priced automobile, not a hyper-expensive European machine. Packing 70 horsepower, the 314-cid engine could propel a Cadillac motor car to speeds in excess of 60 mph without missing a beat, if a driver could find a suitable place to reach those speeds.

Cadillac's ingenuity didn't end at the engine's eight-cylinder configuration. To keep the power plant cool and efficient, a new water system was developed. In addition to large water passages and healthy-breathing exhaust manifolds, thermostatic control of water flow regulated when water could pass through a valve in the water pump and then into the radiator. Like so many other Cadillac technological innovations, the system was widely copied by the industry.

Cadillac engineers were not content to rest on their laurels. While the V-8 was a fine and smooth-running engine that stacked up well against its competitors, it did produce a vibration at 40 to 50 mph that was especially noticeable in increasingly popular closed cars. Many other fine automobiles shared similar characteristics, but Charles Kettering wanted to know why the annoyance was inherent in the V-8. Engineers soon learned that because of the 180-

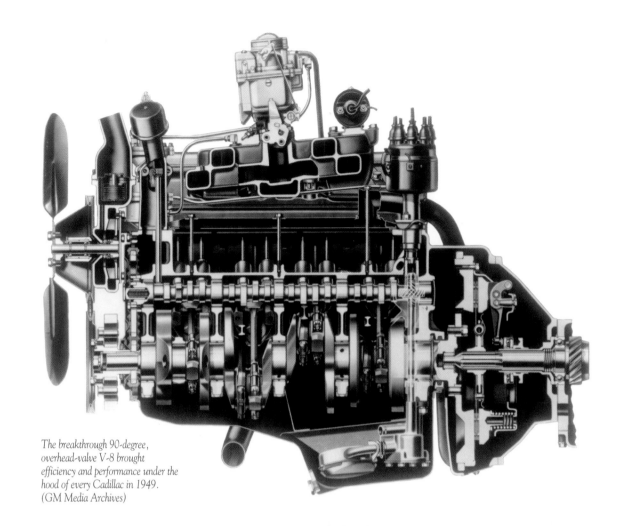

The breakthrough 90-degree, overhead-valve V-8 brought efficiency and performance under the hood of every Cadillac in 1949. (GM Media Archives)

All 1952 Series 62 Cadillacs, including Richard A. Esposito's pictured Series 62 convertible, received the new Dual-Range Hydra-Matic automatic transmission that allowed driver control over third and fourth gears, depending on driving conditions. Saginaw power steering was also available at extra cost for the first time on a Cadillac.

The Panoramic windshield found only on General Motors' premier convertibles, including Cadillac's Eldorado, was a safety innovation that provided more glass area for better viewing. Passengers soon found that the tradeoff with increased visibility came in distortion at the bend of the windshield. Cadillac also introduced the Autronic Eye headlight dimming option in 1953, though this Eldorado does not sport the option. (Jerry Heasley photo)

degree throw each piston traveled and the four-cylinder-type, single-plane crankshaft, the horizontal energy between the pistons battling each other caused the shake from the power plant.

The solution to the engine shimmy was a fully counter-weighted, two-plane crankshaft that balanced the primary and secondary forces from the pistons through properly proportioned weights in the crank itself. The silky-smooth V-8 was introduced on the 1924 models, dubbed "V-63s," and the envious industry couldn't help but laud the Cadillac achievement. Even dissenters who publicly questioned Cadillac's production of a V-8 in 1915 hid their tails. Their mudslinging had caused Cadillac to address the viability of the engine through ads that touted the company's "penalty of leadership," and only helped to radiate Cadillac's supremacy and advertise its achievement.

With a smoother engine under the hoods of its motor cars, Cadillac needed to to match an equally smooth transmission to the engine. But an improved gearbox didn't come from Cadillac, it, literally, came to Cadillac. Trained as a hydraulic engineer, Earl A. Thompson developed and held the patent on a clashless transmission that eliminated the need to double clutch when shifting in forward gears. His choice to develop the system on a Cadillac

Safety innovations on the 1954 Cadillacs included a one-touch system for washing and wiping the windshield and a padded instrument panel cover. (GM Media Archives)

The 1957 Cadillac Eldorado Brougham was the ultimate expression of success in the 1950s. A showcase of innovation, the Eldorado Brougham featured an air suspension system, quad headlights, a memory power seat, automatic door locks, and a foot-operated parking brake that automatically released when the transmission was placed in gear. Robert B. Werner is the proud owner of this Dakota Red beauty, Brougham number 107 of 400 built. (Phil Kunz photo)

was presumably because his brother owned a Cadillac dealership in Oregon. Once he was pleased with the design, Thompson drove the Cadillac from the West Coast to Detroit so the transmission could be scrutinized by Cadillac management. After severe testing of Thompson's transmission alongside several other prototype transmissions by Cadillac engineers, Thompson's transmission design, dubbed "Synchro-Mesh," proved superior through its system of cones that matched the rotational speed of gears before they were meshed. It was quickly integrated into the Cadillac and one-year-old LaSalle lines in 1928; shortly after, the industry would follow with their own synchronized transmissions. Cadillac had, once again, proven through accomplishment that the company was driven to meet its "penalty of leadership."

Mechanical conquests from its beginning had proven the Cadillac to be a superior automobile, and with the arrival of Harley Earl's styling coup de'etat, first with the LaSalle in 1927 and subsequently with the father Cadillac brand in 1928, GM had a true luxury leader that was well rounded. Still, stiff competition from numerous other quality luxury cars, including Packard, Pierce-Arrow, and Lincoln, made it difficult for Cadillac to stand apart.

Something was needed to stop motorists in their tracks when they saw a Cadillac thunder down the road. Previously, Cadillac's reputation as a well-built, cutting-edge automobile had been enough, but it wasn't anymore. The excitement Cadillac needed came in late 1929 with the December announcement by Cadillac Motor Company President Lawrence P. Fisher that Cadillac would offer an automobile with a 16-cylinder engine. Shockwaves rippled through the American auto industry and beyond. Competitors were stunned and customers begged the company for more information.

Serious buyers learned the 452-cid V-16 was designed by Cadillac engineer Owen Nacker with a slim 45-degree angle between the cylinder banks and a bore and stroke of 3 x 4 inches. A horsepower rating of 165 units in the overhead-valve V-16 was achieved through the use of hydraulic valve silencers, which found appeal with the most conservative driving enthusiasts.

But it was the ring of "V-16" that made like a siren's call to the curious and instigated visits to the local Cadillac dealer. What curiosity seekers saw first were the magnificent Fleetwood bodies, but the beauty didn't end with the

Cadillac planned to install such notable innovations as disk brakes, fuel injection, and an independent rear suspension on the Eldorado Brougham, but it never happened. (GM Media Archives)

Following the lead set by the Eldorado Brougham the previous year, all Cadillacs adopted the quad headlight system for 1958. (GM Media Archives)

V-16's exterior. A lift of the hood panel not only revealed the world's first V-16 passenger car, but also the world's first styled engine. It was truly a work of art. Cadillac designers made sure that the aura of the V-16's internals were translated to the exterior appearance of the engine. Long, smooth valve covers echoed the V-16's smooth operation, and the rest of the engine was a harmonious blend of aluminum, chrome, enamel, and porcelain worthy of its own display in an art museum alongside other Art Deco works. When crowned

To improve Cadillac ride quality, each member of this fleet of 1959 Cadillacs carried low-pressure, freon-filled shock absorbers. (GM Media Archives)

with a lightweight body and fit with the right rear axle ratio, a V-16 Cadillac bowed only to a straight-eight Model J Duesenberg when it came to performance in 1930. With Cadillac's equally smooth Synchro-Mesh transmission, the rambunctious Duesenberg couldn't compete with the V-16's smoothness or quiet elegance.

To solidify its intentions to dominate the highest rung of the market, Cadillac unveiled a second multi-cylinder car, the V-12, before the end of 1930. The 368-cid 12-cylinder used

When the rear door was opened on 1959 and 1960 Eldorado Broughams, the rear quarter window recessed out of the way and into the sail panel. (Old Cars Weekly photo)

This 1960 Seville coupe, like all 1960 Cadillacs, benefited from new self-adjusting brakes. During this time period, Cadillac was paying increased attention to the brake systems of its automobiles.
(GM Media Archives)

a similar internal and external design and shared mechanical innovations with the V-16. Though four cylinders shy of its behemoth brother, the 12-cylinder also became known for its smooth and quiet operation, and with 135 horsepower, it was likewise known for its power.

In the face of worldwide economic despair, Cadillac trudged on, never forgetting its place as a leader in technology. By 1934, Cadillac was ready to offer two innovations that had been under development for several years: hydraulic brakes and knee-action suspension. While the hydraulic brakes were first applied only on the LaSalle line, the new suspension system was offered on both makes. The trademark smoothness of Cadillac power plants was now mated with smoother riding action through the independent coil spring suspension developed by Maurice Olley, an engineer who had emigrated from Rolls-Royce. This improvement was followed in 1935 with a road-stabilizing innovation that promised to keep a Cadillac or LaSalle body level during turns.

As early as the introduction of the V-8, Cadillac had shown its dedication to providing vehicles that offered the most in comfort, power, and luxury. In 1941,

the company would truly upset the luxury car industry with clutchless shifting. Though not an innovation credited solely to Cadillac, it did offer what Packard, Chrysler, and Lincoln, Cadillac's few remaining competitors, could not.

Dubbed "Hydra-Matic," the automatic transmission had first been offered in the Oldsmobile line during 1940, and in 1941 it became optional on a new Cadillac. For the second time in less than 15 years, Cadillac had proven its ability to make a uniquely smooth, powerful automobile.

While it was a relatively dependable innovation, there were a few bugs to work out of the transmission. Cadillac had the opportunity to handle the task when it was summoned to produce tanks for the United States government in World War II. M-5 and M-24 Chaffee tanks, among others, were produced at Cadillac's Clark Street production facility using two Cadillac 346-cid V-8s, each backed by a Hydra-Matic transmission. If there was ever a way to test the durability of a power plant and its accessories, it was in the belly of a beastly tank under the direction of a frenzied soldier under attack. The combinations

Cadillac was the first manufacturer to adopt cornering lights, and all of its 1962 models carried them. (GM Media Archives)

proved successful in the war effort, but Cadillac continued improving the setup's dependability and efficiency throughout the war, and by the time peace came, the system had been perfected for passenger cars.

Poised to establish itself in the fresh postwar automotive market, Cadillac dropped another technological bomb in 1949, and the automotive world would again be forever different. Once again, Cadillac was ready to set the pace with a new V-8, much like it had in 1915 and 1923. Work on this monumental new V-8 began in 1937, when engineers searched for a way to increase the compression of the 346-cid flathead engine to take advantage of more efficient high-octane fuels. Upon discovering the flathead's limitations, engineers looked for other ways to increase the compression ratio to take advantage of the efficient new "wonder fuel."

New innovations on the 1964 Cadillacs included Climate Control temperature setting and Twilight Sentinel lighting features. (GM Media Archives)

Cadillac engineers, under the supervision of John Gordon, Harry Barr, and Edward Cole, designed an overhead-valve engine that ran smoothly under the stresses of compression ratios above 8:1, thanks to slipper-style pistons designed by piston specialist Byron Ellis. The skirting allowed the engine to run lighter pistons, and with shorter rods, thanks to a compressed path of travel. The pistons were arranged 90 degrees apart and traveled efficiently in chorus through wedge-shaped chambers.

The result of their work in 1949 was a cleaner-looking and lighter V-8 that sipped less fuel, produced more power, and did it all in less engine displacement. Best of all, there was room for more power through higher compression ratios, and Cadillac would need it. Its engine started a horsepower boom that was reinforced by an engine of similar design offered by Oldsmobile that same inaugural year.

Media accolades quickly followed from *Life*, *The Motor*, and *Motor Trend*, which

awarded the Cadillac the first of its annual coveted "Car of the Year" honors. Through imitation, the design also earned respect from the rest of the industry as other automakers used blueprints of the engine's design for their own cars. Cadillac had once again chartered the future.

In the field, the Cadillac overhead-valve V-8 proved itself at the Le Mans 24 Hours in the hands of Briggs Cunningham, who fielded two 1950 Cadillac Series 61s. The first car was stock, save for a few race-required alterations. The second was a Series 61 with a highly modified aerodynamic body. The stock coupe finished first in its class and 10th overall with the special-bodied "Le Monstre" taking 11th overall. Like its predecessor, Cadillac's new power plant also found its way into tanks, this time in the Korean War. It, too, proved its worth on the battlefield.

All 1969 Cadillacs received the industry's first closed cooling system that recovered lost anti-freeze in the event of boil-over. (GM Media Archives)

Almost annual boosts were given to the horsepower rating of the overhead-valve V-8 through increased compression ratios and the addition of dual exhaust systems and four-barrel carburetors. This sparked safety concerns, and Cadillac was prepared to answer them with fresh innovations. In 1953, a spacecraft-looking headlight dimmer landed on the option list. The unit, named the "Autronic Eye," was mounted on the driver's side of the dashboard, and during nighttime driving sensed an oncoming car's headlights. The dimmer would then automatically turn the high beams off, then turn them on again

when the car had passed. By 1954, the dimmer could be placed atop a padded dashboard that increased passenger safety in a crash.

Safety continued on the outside with a new one-touch windshield washing system that squirted washer solvent onto the windshield and automatically started the wipers. This one-step process allowed a driver to concentrate on the task at hand—driving—without fumbling through controls. The innovative system was relegated to duties on another General Motors innovation—the

Panoramic windshield. Introduced on the Chevrolet Corvette, Oldsmobile Fiesta, Buick Skylark, and Cadillac Eldorado dream cars at the 1953 Motorama, the Panoramic made its first regular production showing on the 1954 Cadillacs and Buicks. More than just a styling exercise that added beauty, the wrap-around windshield increased the glass area for added safety.

Technology was rapidly developing through the 1950s, and advancements weren't limited to mechanical parts. Automotive design and luxury were adding to the driving experience, but were often limited to show cars. Cadillac brought a little of that future to the customer when it released its technology-laden Eldorado Brougham to the public. Itself derived from a show car, the Brougham featured all of Cadillac's latest innovations, many not found even on a deVille or top-of-the-line 1957 Eldorado Biarritz or Seville. A low, brushed stainless-steel roof and suicide-style pillarless hardtop doors that didn't require a center pillar to latch were just a few of the features that justified the car's astronomical $13,074 price tag.

The Eldorado Brougham rode on an air-ride suspension system that floated over the bumps and an anti-dive feature that kept the car's nose from biting at the ground when the car came to a halt. When the driver turned the ignition to the "on" position, the car automatically started when the car was placed in park or neutral. It also featured a quad headlight system that would be the industry norm the following year.

At $13,000-plus for each Brougham, technology had a price. Cadillac shared in the expense and reportedly lost around $10,000 for each Brougham it produced, but the purpose of the Brougham was not to turn a profit. Rather, it was to demonstrate the luxury carmaker's might and prove its leadership in the industry. But the Brougham did more than that. It greased the way for the upcoming decades by introducing many trends. Like the Brougham, Cadillacs of the '60s would get much lower in design, and conveniences aimed at pleasing the driver would increase.

Driver convenience was maximized in 1964 with the introduction of two innovations that would find their way into Cadillacs for decades: Twilight Sentinel and Comfort Control. Bringing the luxuries of home into the automobile had been a goal of automakers since the first couch-like seat was installed in a motor car. That pursuit continued with the first thermostatically regulated heating, cooling, and ventilating system in 1964 models. The unit worked much like a home thermostat and would turn on the air conditioner or heater, whichever was required to meet the driver's desired temperature.

The restyled 1974 Cadillacs, along with some Buick and Oldsmobile models, could be ordered with the innovative air cushion restraint system to protect the driver in the event of a head-on collision. The system didn't find immediate popularity, but a resurgence in safety concerns made the system a government-mandated standard feature on all automobiles by the 1990s.

The 1970 Fleetwood Eldorado was originally selected to be the bearer of the largest passenger-car engine (500 horsepower, 400 cid) to ever beat beneath the hood of an automobile. By 1975, the year this Fleetwood Eldorado hails from, the personal luxury model had to share its engine with the rest of the full-size Cadillac lineup. (GM Media Archives)

Safety was taken another step with the addition of the optional Twilight Sentinel, which automatically turned headlights on at dusk and off at dawn. The lighting addition complemented Cadillac's pioneering cornering lamps beginning in 1962. The next year, Cadillac added driver comfort through its optional tilt and telescopic steering wheel.

Throughout the 1960s, Cadillac power plants (and those around the industry) continued to be based upon the overhead-valve design of 1949. Evolution caused the engine to grow in size, power, and efficiency, but Cadillacs were no longer known for their tire-screaming performance. That was left to the growing muscle car segment that encouraged corporations to dump powerful engines into the lightest car in a company's catalog. Cadillac took the high road and continued to build the large cars Americans expected from the company.

Growing emphasis on safety and comfort became Cadillac's primary object, but in 1967, the company was able to feed its appetite for a personal car that combined safety and technology with the strong-hearted performance for which it was known.

A new Eldorado personal coupe with the aggressive lines and profile of the youthful muscle cars gave Cadillac a new place to feature fresh technology, all the while retaining its prestigious identity. Underneath the Eldorado's tailored body creases lay a hotbed of innovation in the front-wheel-drive system.

Beaten by one year with Oldsmobile's Toronado, the 1967 Eldorado wasn't the first mass-produced front-wheel-drive General Motors automobile, but it had its own flavor. Under the Eldorado's hood purred the 429-cid V-8 found in the rest

Cadillac saved the best for last with its two-seat grand finale of the 1990s, the 1993 Allanté. The innovative Northstar V-8 engine was only available in the Allanté during the car's final year of production, making these 1993 models the most sought after.

*In the early 1980s, Cadillac offered beautiful exteriors on its designs, but its V-8-6-4 was a disappointment, and the 4.1-liter V-6 and V-8 engines didn't provide adequate power for the size of the cars.
(GM Media Archives)*

of the Cadillac line, but modifications had to be made in order to make the engine power the front wheels. To do so, Cadillac and Borg-Warner developed an ingenious drive chain to power the axles from the side-positioned Turbo Hydra-Matic transmission. The system proved to be durable and kept the popular Eldorado on the cutting edge.

Computer technology continued its rapid growth in the 1970s, and Cadillac safety and comfort were the benefactors. Some of the innovations were far ahead of their time and found a brief life in the decade in which they were created, only to be re-introduced decades later throughout the industry under

government mandate. The first of these innovations was Track Master, a computerized anti-lock rear brake system. Three years later, an air-cushion restraint system shared with Buick and Oldsmobile was offered on Cadillacs at extra cost. Like today's air bags, Cadillac's system cushioned the impact of a front-end collision. Computer-aided electronics again brought the future into Cadillac's hands with the introduction of electronic fuel injection on the mighty 500-cid V-8 now powering all large Cadillac models, from the Eldorado to the deVille. Cadillac was not the first American car company to offer electronic fuel injection, but it was the first to employ it with success. The Cadillac Seville harnessed digital electronic computer control in 1978 with a trip computer. Just two years later, computer technology would be at work in Cadillac's ignition and fuel-injection systems, and even work as a brain to diagnose engine functions.

The application of computer technology took a step back for a brief moment in Cadillac history with the arrival of the 6.0-liter engine Cadillac dubbed the "V-8-6-4." Available at the end of 1980, the engine was built to run on a varying number of cylinders, the number depending on the amount of load the engine was under. When under the stress of heavy acceleration, the engine operated under all eight cylinders. When loads and stress on the engine lightened, the engine would shut down cylinders in pairs via solenoids that blocked engine valves, thus saving fuel—in theory. In reality, the system gave the Cadillac engine an uncommon roughness, and that was when it was running properly. The idea has not been lost to the history books, however. Several

Cadillac pioneered the first transverse-mounted V-8 engine in a front-wheel-drive automobile in 1985. The system Cadillac used included an advanced viscous-damped, torque converter clutch.

Cadillac's study in aerodynamics in the late 1980s produced these concept cars—the 1988 Voyage (left) and the 1989 Solitaire. The Voyage was designed for stability at 200 mph, and both cars featured hands-free cellular phones. The Solitaire in the background was powered by a 6.6-liter port-injected engine rated at 430 horsepower that was produced in conjunction with Lotus. (GM Media Archives)

manufacturers, including Cadillac, have since revisited the principles of the system in hopes of providing both V-8 power and exceptional fuel economy.

Thanks to the innovations of the Eldorado's front-wheel-drive system and the following popularity of the system in competitive makes, customers began seeking front-wheel-drive cars in force by the 1980s. To answer the demand, Cadillac's freshly downsized, bread-and-butter deVille line adopted the system in 1985. Always thinking ahead, the company added a twist to its engine layout and became the first American car company to arrange a V-8 in a transverse fashion. This put the transmission in line with the V-8's crankshaft, and allowed the use of a unique viscous-damped torque converter clutch. The sporty two-seat Allanté took the transverse-mounted engine layout one step further with its electronic traction control feature. By reducing engine power and adjusting each individual front brake, the traction control system kept an Allanté and its driver in control under stress.

As the premium automobile in Cadillac's impressive lineup, the Pininfarina-built Allanté served as Cadillac's showcase for innovation. In 1993, the Allanté, along with the Seville Touring Sedan, introduced Cadillac's greatest technology of the decade: the Northstar engine. A 32-valve, 4.6-liter powerhouse, the Northstar delivered "leading-edge performance with unparalleled smoothness, luxury and control," according to the company. From its birth, the heart of a Cadillac was its engine, and with the Northstar, a new pulse surged back into the company. Cadillac was back on the throne that it had created.

Cadillac noted that the Northstar engine was "the result of an intensive, four-year development process designed to set new standards for the world in refinement and performance, quality and reliability, and quiet, smooth operation." Though quiet, the 290-horsepower engine screamed to be driven, and the sporty Allanté and Seville Touring Sedan were a perfect fit. The robust, all-aluminum 4.6-liter Northstar engine in both the Allanté and Seville Touring Sedan was part of a system that included a sophisticated ride control

system dubbed "Road Sensing Suspension," speed-sensitive steering, and continued use of a traction-control system.

A smooth ride was guaranteed through the high-speed computer in the Road Sensing Suspension system, which determined the damping requirements every millisecond. For aggressive driving needs, the system also made the ride firmer when the computer determined it was necessary. Only three years later, the Road Sensing Suspension system was upgraded to allow "an infinite range of settings, from boulevard soft to race car firm."

Using thermal imaging technology gained after Operation Desert Storm, Cadillac introduced the Night Vision system on 2000 DeVilles, which allowed drivers to see beyond the range of their headlights at night for added safety. (GM Media Archives)

The OnStar in-vehicle communication device served to protect and aid Cadillac owners in the event of an emergency and was first available on Cadillacs in 1997. The option continued through 1998, the year of this Cadillac DeVille D'Elegance model.

Formal, but luxurious. Sporty, yet elegant. The 2001 DeVille cloaked in black thunders down a stretch of road. (GM Media Archives)

Also introduced in 1996, the technologically driven Magnasteer system tailored steering controls to a driver's speed and allowed a set amount of steering assist to the driver for maximum safety and driving pleasure.

Cadillac's commitment to its customers continued with the 1997 introduction of OnStar, a communication device that combined the benefits of Global Positioning Systems with cellular phone technology. Emergency situations, navigation instructions, and other driver needs were just a button push away from a 24-hour, 365-day customer service center. Concierge services even include unlocking a Cadillac's doors for a marooned driver.

StabiliTrak also debuted in 1997, adding to the Cadillac driving experience by ensuring more secure handling during cornering and emergency maneuvers. A yaw rate sensor and a lateral acceleration sensor read the actions of the car's suspension, steering, and anti-lock braking system to increase driver control.

Added driver safety brought Cadillac into the new millennium in 2000 with the infrared Night Vision system, cleverly disguised in the grille of the redesigned Deville. Using technology employed by American and Coalition forces in the Persian Gulf War, a Deville driver could detect road hazards beyond the range of the car's headlights in the cloak of nightfall. Additional sensing controls were employed in the Ultrasonic Rear Park Assist system, which was capable of sensing objects through sensors in order to prevent driver-instigated collisions.

Cadillac has poised itself for continued leadership in technology with the upcoming V-Series luxury automobiles through even higher levels of engine and suspension performance together with improved braking characteristics. Stay tuned—it's going to be a smooth, brisk ride.

Night Vision systems used in the Gulf War were employed in the LMP race cars to aid in night driving. (Cadillac Historical Collection)

Style

No American automobile has more of a history with style than Cadillac. Before developing the manner in which the exterior of cars are designed, Cadillac put flavor into its products, beginning with the tulip-shaped bodies of the 1906 Models M and K. Already a flower among weeds, the tulip-bodied passenger compartments of these early Cadillacs hinted at the development for which Cadillac would be known.

As early as 1905, Henry Leland was probing the future of automobile design and comfort when he had the industry's first concept car built to test the feasibility of adding a closed body style to the Cadillac catalog in late 1905. Born from Leland's test was Osceola—a tall, closed-coupe automobile that took the name of a Seminole Indian chief.

100 Years

The 1928 Cadillacs were the first to receive the styling touch of Harley Earl. After drawing up the Hispano-Suiza-influenced LaSalles, Earl applied the same successful front ensemble to the Cadillac line, including this Series 341 convertible coupe. (GM Media Archives)

Osceola's tulip-shaped passenger compartment was used on Model M and K Cadillacs the following year, but Osceola added a top-heavy telephone booth-shaped roof and cowl. Pleased with the results, Leland made the body style available to Cadillac customers in 1906, but it was expensive at $3,000. In 1910, Cadillac became the first company to offer closed bodies as standard catalog offerings.

Through the 1910s and 1920s, cars generally grew rounder and displayed pleasingly smoother lines, but there were few dramatic differences between makes as automakers followed similar parameters when designing their cars. Unique touches and exotic body designs were left to the custom body houses, and such changes came at a great price. Just as they had from the beginning, mechanical engineers continued to dictate the outward design of automobiles during this period to make the most efficient use of the drive train layout. This engineer-based method of dressing the automobile for business was challenged by Cadillac in the mid 1920s. And rather than be threatened by this step on their turf, custom body houses found themselves the benefactors.

In its quest to create a companion Cadillac marque, General Motors forever changed the entire way it, and its competition, viewed the role of a car's design and those artisans behind it. Shortly after becoming president of the Cadillac Motor Car Division in 1925, Larry Fisher, of the body-building Fisher company, was given the task of adding the new, lesser-priced LaSalle. A review of several in-house designs for the LaSalle left Fisher unmoved, so he called Harley Earl, a

This emblem was likely applied to custom-bodied Cadillac creations. (GM Media Archives)

young California designer whose custom body creations for wealthy Californians and the Hollywood set had been fetching the attention of GM brass. Earl's designs were coming out of Earl Auto Works, a business his father owned until selling out to Don Lee, the owner of several majestic Cadillac franchises along the West Coast. Lee kept Harley Earl on after his purchase as a custom body designer, but Earl also played the part of salesman by displaying his renderings to the area's selective clientele in clay—his favored three-dimensional medium.

Counted among Earl's customers were the area's wealthy, some of whom had

Harley Earl is often toasted as the man responsible for General Motors' superior styling, beginning with the 1927 LaSalle and ending with the 1958 models. Recent advertisements have hailed Earl as "The da Vinci of Detroit." (Cadillac Historical Collection)

The man responsible for the beautiful Cadillacs and LaSalles of the 1930s through the 1950s, Harley Earl, sits in the car that got him hired at General Motors, the 1927 LaSalle. Cadillac chief Lawrence Fisher can be seen standing behind the LaSalle Series 303 roadster. (GM Media Archives)

Instead of leading Cadillac design as it had following its 1927 introduction, the LaSalle began following Cadillac design by 1931. Like all 1931 LaSalles, this convertible coupe borrows the Cadillac V-16's grille screen and hood vent doors. (Jerry Heasley photo)

found new riches by acting on the silver screen and wanted to display their good fortune by being seen in personalized one-of-a-kind automobiles. Earl built up a healthy business by drawing customers through outgoing cars painted in vivid hues.

The attention didn't go unnoticed by Cadillac division president Larry Fisher's brother, Fred, who was acquainted with Earl and his method through a country club. When Larry Fisher exhausted the design talents of his own staff in the creation of the LaSalle, he turned to Earl as a last resort.

Earl brought his trademark dazzle and imagination to Cadillac's Clark Street plant and immediately began work with Cadillac body engineers Dave Anderson and Ralph Pew, and master woodworker and clay modeler Jack Parks. Long an admirer of the agile lines of the French-built Hispano-Suizas, Earl drew inspiration from them and created an original and exceedingly beautiful design for the LaSalle of his own suggestion.

A blackboard drawing of the 1932 Cadillac all-weather phaeton. (GM Media Archives)

Seeing the car on paper was one thing, but Earl knew that to appreciate the design of the car, a scale version had to be presented before GM brass. Clay models of a touring car, a four-door sedan, a coupe, and a rumble seat roadster were prepared for Alfred Sloan and Larry and Fred Fisher. Earl's clay LaSalles won over Sloan and the Fishers, and accolades from customers and the critics followed once the LaSalle was released. Almost immediately after, Earl was directed to work that same magic on the entire GM lineup through the newly created Art & Colour Department. From this point on, automobiles within GM would be designed by artists. Some of the 20th century's most beautiful automobiles were about to fill glass-faced dealer showrooms, thanks to Harley Earl and his LaSalle.

Cadillac was next to benefit from Earl's pen, and the 1928 models were adorned with the same Hispano-Suiza influences, particularly noticeable in the grille and large headlights. While the Earl-designed 1927 LaSalles and 1928 Cadillacs were beautiful cars in their own right, it was the Fleetwood bodies for a super-secret V-16 series of Cadillacs in 1930 that marked a new brand of Cadillac style. Previously, mechanical engineers designed an automobile's sheet metal around its mechanical components. With the V-16, artists styled the engine to be as beautiful as the metal around it.

The 1932 models were among the most beautiful cars to roll out of the Cadillac plant in the Classic era, from V-8 to V-16. Sweeping fenders, a tall and narrow grille shell without a screen, and details like wind splits on the headlights, taillights, and parking lamps made the 1932 models stand out in the field of luxury offerings. (GM Media Archives)

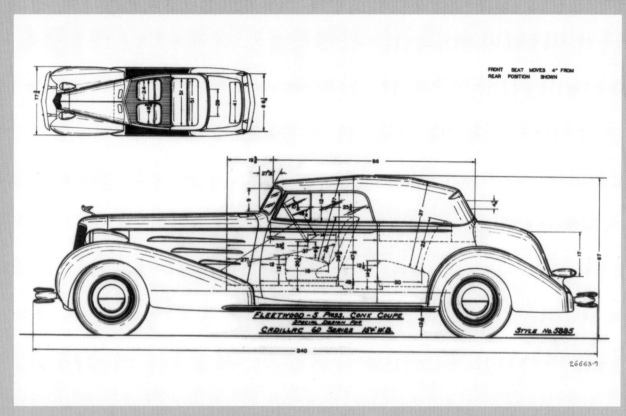

A designer put a lot of work into sketching out the dimensions of the 1934 Cadillac Fleetwood five-passenger convertible coupe on the Series 452 V-16 chassis, but alas, only one was sold that year. (GM Media Archives).

Long, black valve covers capped off the enamel-coated engine for an understated elegance that was unmatched by any other automobile at the time. So clean was the engine compartment that not even a stringy spark plug wire was visible. Similar attention under the hood was paid to the like-styled V-12 Cadillacs of 1931. The beautiful engines added to the aura of both models and helped Cadillac establish its intentions of being a contender in the ultra-luxury class of automobiles.

The majestic V-16s earned admiration throughout the industry through an imposing grille and radiator protected by a chrome mesh screen. Large headlights flanked the grille and were

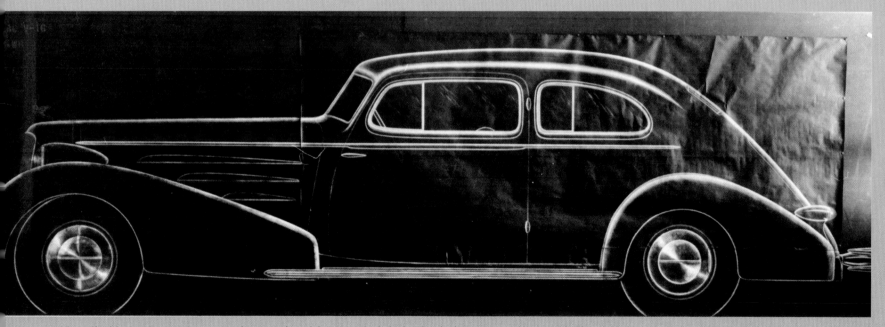

The profile of the Aero-Dynamic Coupe was truly cutting-edge and, by 1934, a few bodies based on the show car were trickling out of the Fleetwood body company's doors. (GM Media Archives)

bridged by a bar, upon which the awesome engine's presence was announced with a V-16 emblem. Buyers had a wide choice of semi-custom Fleetwood body styles from which to choose—all of which had been approved by Earl himself. Of all the Fleetwood bodies, the Fleetwood-built Madame X bodies are the most mysterious and fascinating, much like the main character in the Broadway play Earl named the special series for. These especially elegant closed-body cars were tailored with a straight sill, thin chrome window frames, and a horizontal belt molding. Even today, the draw of the Madame X bodies is profound.

Streamlining cues fascinated artists, and their impressions of the design techniques were soon found on everything from trains to buildings to furniture. Thanks to the artists, these influences soon found their way into automobile design. Skirted fenders quickly made their mark on the entire Cadillac lineup, and speed lines nestled their way onto the fender skirting and hood sides of luxurious V-16 models in 1933. An additional ode to the Art Deco movement

Although it carries the Madam X-style windshield and chrome window frames, the body number on this Series 452 V-16 coupe for two passengers was not listed in the 4100 series, but rather is a Series 4476 straight sill coupe. (GM Media Archives)

GM's Art & Colour department is shown working on dashboards and the 1934 LaSalle sedan. (GM Media Archives)

was found in the bumper, which was composed of four thin, parallel, chrome bars.

Cadillac set the stage for the future of automotive design at the 1933 Chicago Century of Progress Exposition with its futuristic V-16 Aerodynamic Coupe. The commanding coupe sported a slick fastback roof design and pontoon fenders that echoed the car's profile. Its defining styling features were widely copied on successive GM products, and even influenced competing makes (most notably the innovative front-wheel-drive Cord, the art piece of designer Gordon Buehrig). So striking was the show car that Cadillac added it to the line on a special-order basis and at least 20 were built on V-8, V-12, and V-16 chassis.

Never a popular body style in the United States, the convertible Victoria also found limited success in the Cadillac V-16 line. Only two were built in 1935.

Styling proved it could do more than attract customers to the Cadillac and LaSalle brands, it could also save a marque. The LaSalle enjoyed a successful inaugural year, but sales quickly grew dismal by the early 1930s, and corporate figures were preparing to axe the junior Cadillac. The Depression was taking its toll on the industry, and GM had already pared down its catalog of makes by eliminating the slow-selling Viking and Marquette brands. Upon hearing that his favored LaSalle would likely suffer extinction itself, Earl stepped in and enlisted the help of designer Jules Agramonte. With Earl away, Agramonte designed a sleek

Once seeing this car "in the tin," it's difficult to understand why this dashing Fleetwood dual-cowl sport phaeton proposal based on the 1934 V-16 chassis was unable to attract any orders. The body on this 1935 Cadillac V-16 is a modern recreation of the unbuilt proposal in the 1934 catalog. (Old Cars Weekly archives)

Cadillac maintained strict control over the bodies mounted on its chassis, leaving much of the coachwork to Fleetwood for its cataloged semi-custom bodies, but this eight-cylinder Series 75 chassis escaped into the hands of famous coachbuilder Rollston, who was known for its very formal passenger compartment exterior designs. The company mounted this single town car body on a 1937 Cadillac chassis. Of particular note are the painted hubcaps and wheel covers. (Old Cars Weekly archives)

automobile that borrowed from the Art Deco school of styling, the fashion of sand-eating European racecars, and the Aerodynamic Coupe show car.

The result was purely LaSalle, but with a modern edge. A tall, ribbed grille borrowed from the racecars was walled by pontoon-like fenders from the Aerodynamic Coupe. Art Deco portholes on the hood sides and bi-plane bumpers bookcasing the LaSalle's round lines screamed speed and spoke the future.

After a sample body was hurriedly produced, Earl presented the LaSalle before GM big wigs and declared, "Gentlemen, if you decide to discontinue the LaSalle, this is the car you're not going to build,"

This 1937 LaSalle showed the continued use of the tall, narrow grille that designer Jules Agramonte borrowed from track and beach racers when first styling the 1934 LaSalles.

The Hollywood, California coachbuilding firm Coachcraft, Ltd. opened its Melrose Avenue business in 1940 to serve the needs of local Angelinos and the silver screen set. The company turned out many Cadillac-based custom jobs for customers, including this interesting trio comprised of a 1946 sedan with suitcase fenders and special roof treatment, a unique 1941 two-door woodie wagon, and a low and personalized 1947 coupe. The woodie in the center was built for cowboy actor Charles Starrett, who used it to rest in while shooting western films. (A. Ward Shanen photo; Angelo Van Bogart collection)

according to Micheal Lamm and Dave Holls in their book *A Century of Automotive Style*. "The audience applauded when the parted curtains revealed Agramonte's handsome design, and an extended life was granted to the junior Cadillac.

The LaSalle would use the tall, thin grille as its trademark until its demise in 1940. But before it passed into history, the LaSalle would predict style one final time.

Intending to design a new LaSalle, Bill Mitchell, a freshly hired young designer, drafted an automobile that married styling cues from expensive coach-built

Coachbuilder Derham Custom Body Company built this single town car with a ladaulet-style roof over the rear seat. Modifications to the Cadillac are extensive, from the cowl rearward, but the classic 1941 Cadillac tombstone grille and suitcase front fenders have been preserved in their factory form.

Cadillac was one of the first companies to unveil new postwar designs in 1948. Because of the changeover, new Cadillacs didn't begin rolling off the Clark Street plant in Detroit until February, 1948. (GM Media Archives)

The influence of war extended to automobile design, most visibly on the finned 1948 Cadillacs, which borrowed styling cues from the P-38 fighter plane. This 1948 Series 62 coupe, often referred to as a Sedanette, is posed with a periord aircraft. (GM Media Archives)

cars with a purely Cadillac body. Mitchell's proposed LaSalle had a gentle, romantic, coupe-style torpedo rear deck with an intimate, close-coupled passenger compartment with inviting arched window pillars reaching into the stately roof. The elimination of running boards between suitcase-style fenders brought the car an aire of the future and guaranteed its addition to the Cadillac line for 1938. The wildly different design earned a new designation: "Sixty Special." So innovative was the style that its cues were soon found across the board on GM's sedans beginning in 1940.

Today, many collectors believe the zenith in Sixty Special design was reached when a wide, tombstone-shaped, egg-crate grille perfectly matched to the theme of the sedan graced the nose of the 1941 models.

In addition to the wide grille, all 1941 Cadillacs displayed a pronounced width to their design without looking excessively heavy. Single headlights widely polarized at the ends of the front fenders emphasized the new low look that soon influenced automobile design far beyond Cadillac.

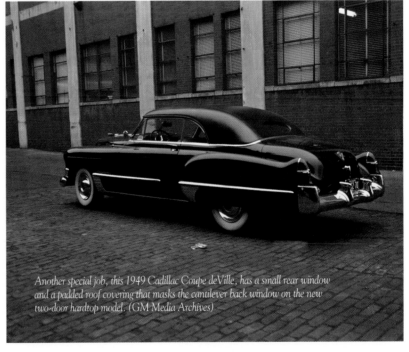

Another special job, this 1949 Cadillac Coupe deVille, has a small rear window and a padded roof covering that masks the cantilever back window on the new two-door hardtop model. (GM Media Archives)

Arriving at the office or the country club in a Cadillac spoke of taste and culture to an owner's peers. An owner, like his Cadillac, had a clear appreciation for forward thinking and a desire for leadership. Cadillac had lived up to this attitude, if not created it, in the motoring world.

Still more Cadillac elegance arrived with new, decidedly wide models in 1942. These showed a clearer break from the tall grille, which had once doubled as a radiator. In its place was a low, wide, egg-crate-styled grille that allowed air to feed a powerful and reliable flathead engine. Thunderous fenders swept the sides of the Cadillac, adding a graceful width for a low and wide stance. The racy fastback styling first displayed on the Aerodynamic Coupe was added to Cadillac models by 1941 and perfected further on the rounder 1942 models. With production cut short by World War II, the bulbous 1942 design proudly kept Cadillac in a position of styling leadership, but there was an exciting revolution on the horizon that would reflect a new, more flamboyant attitude in the postwar boom.

In 1941, Cadillac designers visited the Selfridge Field military base outside of Detroit, Michigan. Harley Earl arranged the visit for his designers to study the top-secret, twin-tail boom P-38 fighter plane. Rapid developments in aerospace technology meant planes were becoming more efficient, and attention to aerodynamics spurred visually exciting designs. Earl wanted his designers to take away ideas that could be transferred from flight into automobile design. And take away ideas they did.

Back in the studio, the P-38's glass cockpit evolved into a wild passenger compartment with wide booms sandwiching the heavily rounded seating area. Lighter cabins with increased glass area marked many of the designs, but it was the twin booms with their dramatic rear humps that garnered the designers' attention most of all, since it was easy to see them applied to the sides of an automobile.

Cadillac sprung the P-38-influenced design on the new 1948 models, and dealers were dismayed. The flamboyant features were not a part of the stately package a Cadillac customer expected to purchase, or so the dealers thought. But the world was rapidly changing as a youthful excitement took over following victory in Europe and the Pacific. Gaining an appreciation for the luxuries that were taken away during the war effort, Americans were ready to exercise their economic buying power in a robust economy. And for some, indulging in new pleasures and renewing old ones meant adding a Cadillac to the garage.

This 1949 Fleetwood Coupe deVille hinted at Cadillac's upcoming new body style, the two-door hardtop, which wouldn't be released until mid-year. This show car was displayed at the Waldorf Astoria and used a far different two-door hardtop style than the production cars that followed it. (GM Media Archives)

General Motors would design custom automobiles for company executives and celebrities. This car appears to be based on a 1949 Cadillac Fleetwood Sixty Special, but has been given special treatments to the roof with a padded top, a small oval rear window reminiscent of Derham jobs, and arched window frames in the doors. (GM Media Archives)

After going without new cars through World War II, and then finding warmed-over 1942 models awaiting them in dealers' lots, the public was longing for a new car that hinted at the future. The finned 1948 Cadillacs didn't just speak the future, they yelled it with their wild new fins. Perhaps because the new finned Cadillac drew inspiration from the aircraft that helped earn an Allied, consumers immediately embraced this nod to the military's tool. It's more likely, however, that the new attention granted to the rear of an automobile was an exciting idea. Either way, the worries of dealers were quickly eradicated when positive feedback of the design followed the car's introduction.

There were still a few vocal detractors, but their gripes were mainly limited to the fins, for before them lay an entirely new body that exuded sleek, low lines,

One-piece windshields and air vents on the leading edge of the rear fenders were just two of the features on the more lithe, restyled 1950 Cadillacs. Don Tretola's pictured Series 61 coupe utilizes a wheelbase shorter than those on the longer Series 62 models.

and a confidence matched only by the Americans that bought them. The egg-crate grille returned with its now-customary broadness, and continued to field the space between the widely separated headlights. A low hood hovered slightly above the tops of the front fenders, whose lines extended the length of the car. With the overhead-valve V-8 replacing the flathead engine, and the industry's first mass-produced hardtop, the Coupe deVille, joining the Cadillac lineup in 1949, the company had a winning package. A poll that year cinched it. More Americans testified that they wanted an overhead-valve, V-8-powered Cadillac or Oldsmobile more than any other new car on the road.

Aircraft influences continued to manifest themselves in Cadillac design on the thoroughly redesigned 1950 Cadillacs with vast expanses of glass around the curved passenger cockpit. Fins made a second appearance on the trailing end of

each Cadillac built, but were preceded by a vertical chrome band around the car's waistline that squeezed the bulbous rear fenders into the body like a hip-accentuating belt around Jane Russell. The broadened nose of the new body jutted out like the proud chest on a college football player, all the while maintaining Cadillac's characteristic low, lithe look. With the package, Cadillac became the top-selling luxury automobile in the world, finally beating out Packard for the honor.

The original 1950 design was perfected three years later in the model's final year with a very special offering: the convertible Eldorado. Introduced before the public at GM's 1953 Motorama show, the elegant Eldorado harmoniously blended a new curved Panoramic windshield, cut-down doors, and a smooth rear deck with a hidden convertible top boot. The package was stunning.

With the help of Harley Earl, Harold R. "Bill" Boyer, the executive vice president in charge of tank production at Cadillac, had this two-seat convertible built by Cadillac's engineering department. Boyer started out with a 1951 Series 61 coupe, had the wheelbase reduced by 10 inches and the height lowered by six inches, and then added 1952 trim parts. Currently, the car is owned by Boyer's granddaughter, Priscilla Roney. (Angelo Van Bogart photo)

The Eldorado, and Cadillac as a whole, showed off its lofty status in society when President-Elect Dwight D. Eisenhower waved to the world through TV from the backseat of a graceful, white Eldorado on the way to his January 1953 inauguration.

Beginning in the 1940s, Cadillac bumpers used bullet-shaped bumper guards to protect their grille work, and by the early 1950s, they began to take on their own styling cues proportionate to their growing size. By 1953, Cadillac's masculine anterior began to show obvious feminine influences through the large chrome guards.

Noticing the guards were gaining their own personality, an unknown source named the bumper protrusions after the busty and beautiful comedian Virginia Ruth Egnor, who went by the name Dagmar while appearing on late-night TV talk show "Broadway Open House." Wherever there were lights and cameras, a Cadillac and its Dagmars could likely be spotted. Political luminaries, distinguished business people, and Hollywood hot shots loved to open their wallets for the chrome flash of a Cadillac.

The flexibility of Cadillac design through the 1950s ensured that rich businessmen could find the dignified style they desired in the Fleetwood Sixty Specials and factory-built limousines. But a colorful palette of vibrant chrome-

Cadillac pulled the first 1953 model off the assembly line and built it into the magnificent Orleans show car. Originally a Coupe deVille, the Orleans was converted into a four-door hardtop with suicide doors and was given a wraparound windshield from the Eldorado. This show car is believed to still exist on the West Coast. (GM Media Archives)

enhancing hues guaranteed attention to the finely styled lines of a Cadillac and reflected the high-end taste of its driver. Whether gliding up to a social gala or whistling through skyscraper-fenced streets for a night on the town, a Cadillac was unmistakable.

Exciting automobile style was breaking new ground and influencing everything from furniture to appliances, and Cadillac was the style leader. It would take the rest of the industry years to catch up to what Harley Earl's Art & Colour Department, renamed General Motors Styling in 1937, was doing in the studio. By 1955, Chrysler and Ford Motor Company unleashed attractive automobiles that copied the Panoramic windshield and light air about the freshly styled Cadillacs and Buicks. But by then, Cadillac was already ahead of them again. Smooth-sided flanks gracing the new-for-1954 Cadillacs showed an imposing grace through the use of the Panoramic windshield and tasteful, restrained chrome applications.

Cadillac had firmly entrenched itself in the postwar era to not only be the car to own, but the car to be like. When a customer walked into a Cadillac dealer and pinpointed the model, color, and options to suit his or her taste, they wanted their Cadillac to reflect their own sense of style and appreciation for technology. There was still no better way to do that than through a beautifully proportioned Cadillac.

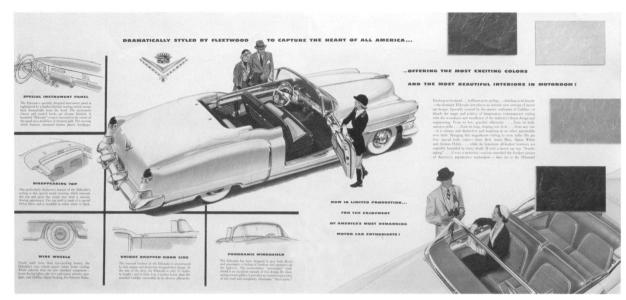

The fine features that made the 1953 Cadillac Eldorado a styling sensation are depicted in this advertisement. (Cadillac Historical Collection)

Cadillac built a pair of two-seat show cars with the revolutionary quad headlight system for the 1954 Motorama—the convertible La Espada and the El Camino coupe (above). Neither made it into production, but the El Camino name showed up on Chevrolet's car-truck hybrid in 1959. (GM Media Archives)

Rich Janis' Fleetwood Sixty Special reflects Cadillac's lower, longer, and wider styling theme that debuted in 1954. That year, every Cadillac received the Panoramic windshield, which added to the wider look. (Angelo Van Bogart photo)

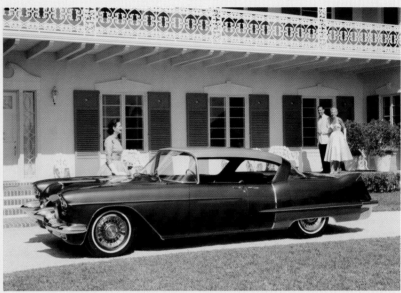

Some of the 1955 Eldorado Brougham show car's innovations included quad headlights, a stainless-steel roof, and air suspension. (GM Media Archives)

The shark fins on the 1955 Cadillac Eldorado predicted the sharper fins that would find their way onto all Cadillac models two years later. (Cadillac Historical Collection)

This styling photo shows that Cadillac toyed with the idea of producing a two-door hardtop companion to the convertible Eldorado model in 1955, but the model wouldn't come to fruition until 1956. A single two-door hardtop Eldorado was also built in 1954 for the president of Reynolds Aluminum. (GM Media Archives)

Bulbous 1953 models gave way to smooth-flanked 1954 Cadillacs that exhibited a cleanness about their well-proportioned bodies. The hood and trunks became fully integrated into the body to complete a smooth transition from the graceful roof to the car's body.

Attention to styling detail was evident in the roof design of these mid-1950s Cadillacs. A Florentine curve to the rear roof pillars swept down and connected the roof to the body of the car. Up front, the aforementioned Panoramic windshield framed the view of the passengers. On sedans, a built-in visor was incorporated.

This body style ranks among Cadillac's most recognizable of the 1950s for all of these features, but thanks to a rising star by the name of Elvis Aaron Presley, they are burned

Above: *The wild fin design of the 1955 Cadillac Eldorado was made even more dramatic with this camera angle.*

Left: *Under the hood of the razor-finned 1955 Cadillac Eldorado convertible lay a dual-carbureted 331-cid V-8 capped by a batwing-shaped air cleaner fitting the car's exterior lines. (GM Media Archives)*

Coachbuilding wasn't dead by the 1950s, but its golden age was certainly over. One of the few companies to still provide custom body features in 1956 was Derham Custom Body Company, which added a padded roof with a small oval rear window to this 1956 Fleetwood Sixty Special. (Angelo Van Bogart photo)

The exclusivity of the Eldorado Brougham would upstage even the most spectacularly accessorized passenger with its stainless-steel top and low, lithe presence. (GM Media Archives)

into the minds of millions of Americans. The king of rock n' roll owned at least three Cadillacs of the 1954-'56 body style: a 1954 Fleetwood Sixty Special, which burned in a fire; a pink 1955 Cadillac Fleetwood Sixty Special he gave to his mother; and a purple 1956 Eldorado Biarritz. The latter two cars are still owned by the Presley estate and continue to remind visitors to Graceland of this handsome era in Cadillac styling.

Presley's Sixty Specials used the smooth fin borrowed from the P-38 fighter plane since 1948 but, on his 1956 Eldorado and all other Eldorados since 1955, the fin began to earn its name. That year, a sharp Eldorado-only shark fin replaced the short, soft fin found on other 1955 models, making the Eldorado sheet metal entirely different. The same separation of fin shape continued through 1956 and, by 1957, every Cadillac had adopted the knife-edge rear fender architecture, from the entry-level Series 62 Cadillac to the elite, super-luxurious Eldorado Brougham. As it had since 1953, the Eldorado continued to share the same grille design up front, but Eldorado again got different fins that made the angular form even sharper through 1958.

By the mid 1950s, everybody was copying Cadillac and paying close attention to their cars' hindquarters. Even economy cars adopted the fin. Being the premier model, the Eldorado set the pace for the gimmick it had started.

Renewed attention to the automobile's anterior end came with the four-headlight system used industry-wide by 1958. The Brougham introduced them to the Cadillac line in 1957 and was one of the first cars to use them and, by the next year, all Cadillacs benefited from the improved lighting setup. The wider headlight arrangement emphasized the growing girth of the Cadillac since 1957, and the industry noticed. Slammed as being too heavy looking, Cadillacs and other 1957 and '58 GM automobiles were compared to the lighter, longer, and

It is believed that three of these 1957 Cadillac Eldorado Seville sedans were built. On the cowl-mounted identification tag on this car, the "Style no." is listed as "non pro," which is believed to mean non-production; no body number or trim number is listed. When John Haferbecker photographed this car, it was owned by Rick Raciborski.

Both of these fashion statements sport flight-worthy attire. To emphasize its style, Cadillac posed fashionable models alongside its latest offerings. Here, a model poses with a 1957 Eldorado Seville. (GM Media Archives)

lower Ford and Chrysler products introduced for the 1957 model year. Although they were certainly attractive in their own right, added bright work was swallowing the otherwise pure lines hiding beneath.

Earl's response to the competition was to add more chrome, but other designers quietly disagreed. When Earl left for Europe during the planning of the 1959

models, the remaining designers drew up cars to match the long and low shapes the competition was using, but they placed special emphasis on a GM trademark — the tail fin.

Tall, airy greenhouses with thin pillars hovered above long and lithe body capsules that were beginning to show the influence of the jet age and space

The influence for Cadillac's fins originally came from the rounded twin booms on the back of the P-38 fighter plane, but by the mid-1950s, they grew sharper and more stylized. The fins on this 1957 Eldorado Biarritz look have lost their P-38 inspiration and look more like dorsal fins poking out through the sea of sheet metal that constitutes the car's trunk. (GM Media Archives)

Every 1957 Cadillac Eldorado, including this Biarritz convertible, received Cadillac's elegant aluminum saber-spoke wheels. The chrome-plated wheels were standard on all Eldorado two-door models from 1955 to 1958, and could be gold anodized in 1956 and 1957. (GM Media Archives)

Cadillac cornered the luxury market by providing models that ranged from very formal, to flashy, to elegant in 1958.

travel. Cadillac owned the wildest and tallest fins of them all in 1959, capped off by a pair of rocket-shaped taillights on each sharp appendage.

Earl was shocked when he returned to see the William "Bill" Mitchell-led designs, but GM President Harlow Curtice supported them and they were approved for production. Earl retired shortly after.

Met equally with awe and criticism, particularly from the funeral car trade that thought the design was anything but distinguished, the extravagant fins became a Cadillac trademark and a defining symbol of the fabulous '50s as a whole.

The 1960 Cadillacs were more restrained than the party-favorite '59s, and it only took subtle changes to the sheet metal to accomplish the new look. The

The silver dome of the General Motors Technical Center hovers behind this 1958 Cadillac Coupe deVille. (GM Media Archives)

added balance to the carved flanks of the 1961 and 1962 models, and were even awarded their own name: skegs.

The low-hanging skegs were short lived and were gone off after the 1962 models. The 1963 models appeared with even lower fins and smoother flanks, losing the mid-fender sculpting marks. A new, serious look came with these cars. The new attitude was due largely to the flatter surfaces that had little of the flamboyance of the 1959 and 1960 Cadillacs.

The state of the nation had always been echoed by Cadillac design, and the changing world of the 1960s shaped a new direction for Cadillac. Political hero John F. Kennedy had been shot and killed, 1950s icon Marilyn Monroe died of a drug overdose, and an added focus on civil rights created an environment of serious deliberation in many people's minds. Cadillac met the challenges of the confused time with designs that appealed to both the prominent and the pleasure seekers. Marked by dignity and greater simplicity, the length of each 1965 Cadillac comprised three planes. A large midsection topped by a shorter stratum that angled up to the roof. Tucking in the flank to the rocker area from the wide midsection was a third flat expanse of metal. Together, these flat surfaces gave the Cadillac shape a new, simplified tune with a renewed harmony throughout its design.

untamed '59s came at the end of and Elvis-influenced, hip-swaying decade, and the 1960s started the martini-swirling, Sinatra-swinging '60s. Dignified designs showed restraint and taste, and catered to both the olive-dunking crowd and Wall Street society.

Sharp lines characterized by the removal of the jet-like taillights and less-pronounced flanks, particularly in the rear fender section, distinguished the 1960s models. A finer grille replaced the three-dimensional bullet pattern found in 1958 and 1959 Cadillacs.

When 1961 rolled around, Bill Mitchell's chiseled design features produced Cadillacs that would carry the company through the early 1960s. Although fins had been shrinking since their apex in 1959, they were not gone as a styling trick. Deciding more is better, though not necessarily at the top of the rear fender, Mitchell's designers explored adding fins to the bottom of the rear fender, as had been done on the Cadillac Cyclone concept car of 1959. The second set of fins

The addition of hash marks on the rocker panels and flanks of the rear license plate of the 1958 Eldorado Biarritz and Seville models was a reflection of Harley Earl's love of chrome. (GM Media Archives)

Bill Mitchell made sure the 1959 General Motors automobiles were longer, lower, and wider. At Cadillac, designer Dave Holls worked Mitchell's theme into the new designs. Holls kept the Cadillac distinct from other GM models by taking the fins to an all-new level. The influence of the jet age can also be seen on this 1959 Eldorado Seville in the bullet taillights and the fuselage-shaped flanks.

An aerial view of the 1959 Cadillac Series 62 convertible shows its almost sinister front ensemble with its bullet grille parts and lurching sheet metal over the headlights. (GM Media Archives)

Black gloves and high heels were as fashionable as the 1957 Cadillac Seville itself. (GM Media Archives)

What Detroit hath wrought: The 1959 Cadillacs were extreme styling adventures that the auto industry has not seen since on a production car. (GM Media Archives)

These royal flanks were capped off at the front with Cadillac's first use of stacked headlights and terminated at the rear with cathedral-style tail lamps that swallowed any remains of the trademark fin. However, their vertical nature served as a reminder to the past and demonstrated Cadillac's continued attention to a car's rear-end design.

The slab sides continued to be a Cadillac trait well into the 1980s and even into the 1990s, but forward-lurching stacked headlights, introduced in 1967, would

The chassis for the 1959 and 1960 Eldorado Broughams were shipped to Turin, Italy, for custom coachwork by Pinin Farina. This 1960 Eldorado Brougham features a lower skeg, a styling feature that would appear on production 1961 and 1962 Cadillacs. (Old Cars Weekly Archives)

only last until the end of the two-year styling cycle Cadillac began practicing in 1957. A fine cross-hatched grille that had been re-introduced in 1960 was again present on the 1967 Calais, deVille, and professional-duty models. The formality of the Cadillac lines was emphasized by a sail panel of matching formality on Coupe deVille and Calais coupes and would be present well into the 1970s.

While they were certainly attractive cars that continued the fine Cadillac styling tradition, the larger sedans were overshadowed by the new Eldorados of 1967. Though the Eldorado was built on GM's first production front-wheel-drive platform, it was the crisp lines (which many compare to the pleats in a fine tailored suit) and the Eldorado's aggressive edges that wowed the industry upon its introducton. That fascination has waned little over time and, even today, the Eldorado draws wonder from automotive novices and connoisseurs alike.

Even with ample room inside, the Eldorados were light-weights compared to the Calais and deVille models. For 1969, the headlights on every Cadillac returned to a side-by-side arrangement, now inset into the grille and out of the dominant

The 1960 Cadillacs featured restrained styling that cleaned up the bullet taillights and pointy chrome teeth jutting out of the grille. (GM Media Archives)

flanks along each body. The immense size of these girthy machines was appealing to Cadillac customers, and they wanted them in record numbers. Amid the polyester and plaid fad, Cadillac steered clear and continued to offer tasteful leathers and ornate cloth patterns inside its cars.

If two fins were great, why not four? Lower fins, or skegs, first appeared on the Pinin Farina-built 1960 Eldorado Broughams and made their way onto all Cadillacs by 1961, the year this Eldorado Biarritz hails from. (GM Media Archives)

A tiara-topped model poses with the freshly chiseled 1961 Cadillac from Bill Mitchell's design studio. (GM Media Archives)

shared. The four-door Seville sedan was Cadillac's top-priced car and was built to compete with European offerings, most notably Mercedes-Benz and Jaguar. Its quad headlight arrangement and egg-crate grille were pure Cadillac, but the squared-off rear end was totally new to the luxury car producer. The success of the Seville made Cadillac a contender in this rapidly growing import car arena.

Threats of oil shortages loomed over the automotive scene through the 1970s and, by 1977, Cadillac was ready to perform some weight-control measures. Aerodynamics were also taken into account when the deVille models were downsized in 1977, amid inklings of further fuel famine. The shorter and smaller Cadillacs retained all of their familiar exterior characteristics, with a four-headlight arrangement, a prominent cross-hatched grille, and flanked sides

Fins were absent from most cars by 1963, but Cadillac continued using them, though they had shrunk from their 1959 high. Ironically, with the disappearance of the lower skegs along the bottom edge, the styling of the 1963 Cadillacs began to include elements that worked on the 1959 and 1960 models, most notably the horizontally bisected grille and the oval rear bumper ends terminating the rocket-inspired flanks. (GM Media Archives)

A merging of the grille and headlight ensemble at the nose of each 1969 Cadillac was the most notable feature of the larger deVille, Calais, and professional chassis and limousine models. Eldorado was also redesigned, but the coupe and convertible models held onto the heavy flanking that began at the leading edge of the front fenders and extended to the rear of the car. The deVille, Calais, limousines, and professional models maintained the flanks, but they were apparent at the terminating edges of the rear fenders.

A turn of styling sparked the 1975 lineup with the addition of the smaller, international-sized Seville model. The first Seville had been a two-door hardtop model based on the design of the 1956 Eldorado, but a formidable price tag (the Seville was more expensive) was one of the only things the 1975 cars really

terminating with continued use of tall, slender taillights built into the ends of the rear bumper. Though smaller on the outside, the new Cadillacs actually had increased interior room. A smaller, downsized Eldorado joined the shrunken Cadillac line two years later.

Heading into the 1980s, a second attempt was made to improve the aerodynamics of the Cadillac, and again the Cadillac design heritage was cleverly retained. An overall wedge shape to the cars was countered by the squarer front-end design that continued to incorporate four headlights surrounding the traditional egg-crate grille. Smaller engines brought better fuel economy and prepared the Cadillac division for a possible fuel crisis. Polarizing Cadillac customers upon its arrival to the 1980 catalog, a new Seville with a unique bustle-back trunk shook up automotive design throughout the industry. Many loved designer Wayne Cady's tribute to the classic automobiles of the 1920s and 1930s, but a seemingly equal number detested the exaggerated Rolls-Royce influence. Regardless of what camp you were in, there was no doubt the design shook up the stagnant art and design trends of the time period.

Function and mechanics began to heavily influence design of all automobiles as front-wheel drive and increased computer technology were sweeping the industry. Smaller cars began to flood the roads, and Cadillac felt pressure to respond. Competing imported makes were smaller than anything Cadillac offered, and the GM division responded with small, front-wheel-drive deVilles in 1985. Present were the telltale Cadillac features, including the vertical sliver taillights and the egg-crate grille, but the prestige and personality of the marque was missing. The cars found plenty of homes, but the soul and spirit from energetic design was gone. Long-time customers, who yearned for the traditional Cadillac, were at least somewhat comforted by the Fleetwood Brougham—the lone full-size, rear-wheel-drive Cadillac remaining.

Realizing that something was missing from the small Cadillac deVille models, the designers added length to the Sedan deVilles and Coupe deVilles by discretely adding extensions to the rear fenders of the unchanged 1985 body shell. Housed in the ends of these rear extension were a pair of traditional vertical taillight lenses, and chrome was tastefully restrained. Cadillac devotees were pleased and Cadillac design was back on track.

Sales of the Sedan deVille increased, but growing appreciation for the convenience of a second pair of doors in the age of the minivan led to dismal sales for the Coupe deVille. By 1993, Cadillac prepared to phase out the deVille after 44 years. Henceforth, customers looking for the personal ambiance and sporty flavor of a two-door luxury coupe from Cadillac were directed to the Eldorado. And it wasn't a bad place to look.

After five years of sharing all of its sheet metal with the lesser-priced Series 62s and deVilles, the 1964 Fleetwood Eldorado received exclusive styling with open rear fenders for a more sporting look that retained the utmost in Cadillac luxury. This 1964 Fleetwood Eldorado was prepared for a GM board of directors showing and wears wheels that didn't make it to production models. (GM Media Archives)

1964 marked the last year fins could be found on the deVille models. The characteristic Cadillac feature would extend one more year on the Seventy Five limousines. (GM Media Archives)

The big news at Cadillac in 1967 was the all-new, front-wheel-drive Fleetwood Eldorado, but across the board Cadillac featured fresh styling that provided a more personal feeling with higher flanks and a low-looking roof as on the Coupe deVille. (GM Media Archives)

The redesigned exterior of the shrunken full-size 1977 Cadillacs was nearing completion when this fiberglass model was photographed. (GM Media Archives)

Fender skirts disappeared and new front lighting changes marked the restyled 1975 Fleetwood Eldorados. Cadillac built 35,802 Fleetwood Eldorado coupes and 8,950 convertibles. The demise of the convertible was near. (GM Media Archives)

John D. Sabo's 1983 Seville features the love-it-or-hate-it bustle-back styling found on Sevilles starting in 1980. Adding classic looks to the classic styling of this Seville is its optional cabriolet roof option.

The Eldorado and Seville suffered from the same lack of Cadillac presence as the deVille when they were restyled in the mid-1980s. Efforts were undertaken to make the top-of-the-line Cadillacs more appealing, but something had to be done to maintain the marque's marketplace integrity, if not the Cadillac brand itself. John O. Grettenberg, working under Design Vice President Chuck Jordan, was ready to make that happen, but the group needed outside help.

Cadillac's jewel in the 1980s, and even into the early 1990s, was the two-seat Allanté, a sports car built to compete with the aging Mercedez-Benz 560SL two-seat sports car. The ingenuity and class built into the now-legendary Allanté made it a lighthouse above the rest of Cadillac design's rocky existence in the late 1980s. Cadillac was ready to employ that beaconing light one last time before the model hit the history books and consulted Pininfarina, the Italian

By 1991, the Cadillac Brougham was showing its age. The model's exterior sheet metal hadn't been changed since 1980.

Cadillac reintroduced the Eldorado convertible in 1984. Like its predecessor, this 1985 Cadillac Eldorado convertible's rear windows rose up and down automatically with the top. (GM Media Archives)

Cadillac's new StabiliTrak system gets put through its paces on a 1997 Cadillac Seville STS. The Eldorado and DeVille also featured the new-for-1997 innovation that provided more secure handling during cornering and emergency maneuvers through a yaw-rate sensor and a lateral acceleration sensor. Together with the Cadillac's suspension, steering, anti-lock brake system, and traction-control system, the sensors determine what the driver intends to do. If the driver doesn't respond as expected, the StabiliTrak computer sends commands to the car's traction control and brakes to keep the car on the intended course.

design studio responsible for the Allanté's appearance. The firm came through with a design, and GM designers melded their own thoughts with that of Pininfarina's and came up with the gorgeous 1992 Eldorado coupe.

Like the Eldorado, the Seville was handsome and worthy of competition with the best international luxury marques. Designers in every market of the industry faced a tough audience in the early 1990s as the computer age spread. Questions arose about how to harness the information age into a pleasing piece of transportation artwork without the corniness of "Number 5," the grotesquely cute robot star of the 1980s film "Short Circuit." The 1992 Eldorado and Seville were a splendid leap forward and even earned respect from relentless critics unable to move beyond Cadillac's shortcomings the previous decade. With the addition of Northstar power a few years later, the pair were unbeatable in the American luxury car market and raised the bar to a new level against their international peers.

Marked by body-colored bumpers that dipped below the Cadillac egg-crate grille, flanked by wide composite headlamps, the Eldorado and Seville dripped of preparedness for the trials of the 1990s. But their styling similarities ended there. The Eldorado flaunted a high rear deck behind its long coupe doors that encapsulated the driver for a uniquely Eldorado personal feel that was further accentuated by thick sail panels. Out back, tall, vertical taillights echoed the Cadillac's heritage.

Just as it had done with the cutting-edge finned 1948 models, Cadillac borrowed styling cues from innovative military aircraft when designing the Stealth Bomber-influenced Cien concept car of 2002. (GM Media Archives)

Seville showed balance with a simply styled sedan roof with sail panels of a smart width. Out back, the now traditional low and wide Seville taillights filled the rear valance and rested above a painted rear bumper. Understated elegance had officially met restless performance ambition.

The fresh look was carried into the new-for-1994 DeVilles through painted bumpers and a general lack of chrome, smooth lines, and an aggressive front ensemble. Now available in sedan form only, the DeVille retained its crimson

sliver taillights and its cross-hatched grille, and found appeal with traditional Cadillac buyers while comparing favorably with competitive offerings.

The industry's largest automobile was still available from Cadillac's stable into the 1990s and appealed very much to the prescribed Cadillac aficionado. Until 1992, the Fleetwood Brougham sedan maintained the same basic body shell first introduced in 1980 with only minor exterior revisions. Against industry assumptions, the car received one last major redesign before it was killed at the

The Sixteen show car was fluidly designed with sharp lines complementing round corners. (GM Media Archives)

end of the 1996 season. Automobile enthusiasts lamenting the introduction of front-wheel drive and yearning for the size of yesterday's automobiles, applauded the large sedan with its generous use of bright work and Cadillac design hallmarks, as well as its traditional rear-wheel-drive/V-8 engine combination. Also pleased were vast numbers of limousine and professional car builders who counted on Cadillac to deliver them beautiful, reliable, and durable cars for their trade.

Revisions to the popular DeVille carried it through the 1990s, until Cadillac prepared an all-new DeVille that could carry the brand into the new millennium. That successor was a truly inspirational sedan with the room of a Cadillac and the look of a stylish competitor. Cadillac gently parted from key features that marked every DeVille before it with wide taillights that maintained their vertical styling feature when illuminated, and headlights that grew square, de-emphasizing the width. A restrained elegance was exhibited in the smooth, ample body sides that blended into the equally understated bumpers. The influence of the successful, and earlier, Seville was clear.

The radical 2002 Cien and 1999 Evoq prototypes display a second direction of Cadillac styling, one that is far more aggressive than the soft lines of the 2000 DeVille. And people are listening. These cutting-edge concepts have the automotive world anxious to learn where Cadillac will take design next.

Ready for rocky passages and paved roadways, Cadillac jumped into the popular SUV market with the Escalade in 1999. The Escalade was an instant hit across all demographics and has already been immortalized in rap music. This 2002 Escalade is dressed in second-generation styling. (Cadillac Historical Collection)

Automotive styling is looking for a leader, and Cadillac is ready with its sharp, angular masterpieces.

The real world test of Cadillac's new styling direction is the CTS, a car with breakthrough design in its chiseled profile and edges. The brand has taken on a mission to blend art and science, and success with this hot performer has new customers walking into their first Cadillac dealerships for a look at the crisply designed sedan.

Following up the CTS is a production version of the Evoq show car, the XLR. The two-seat Cadillac found mass appeal and waiting customers well before it hit the show floor, providing a glowing example of Cadillac's "Art and Science" approach.

Performance

Beating beneath elegantly creased and curved expanses of metal on every Cadillac pulses the heart of the machine. Often overshadowed by the physical beauty of the metal surrounding it, it is the power plant that is the cornerstone of Cadillac's success. From the harmonious one-cylinder engine to the leviathan V-16 and the agile Northstar V-8, Cadillac leadership and innovation has stood the test of time.

It began the moment Henry Leland machined a precision-built engine for Olds Motor Works. Leland's method of manufacture resulted in a more efficient and powerful one-cylinder engine that outperformed the engines of similar design that John and Horace Dodge supplied to Olds.

100 *Years*

Taking the knowledge acquired in building the Olds motor, Leland went to work on a second cylinder with an improved design in mind. That one-cylinder engine became the foundation for the Cadillac Automobile Company and laid a precedent for Cadillac performance.

Realizing the potential of the one-cylinder motor cars, Alonson P. Brush, principle designer behind the new Cadillacs, immediately tested the 10-horsepower engine on the front steps of the Wayne County building in Cadillac Square in the heart of Detroit. Crowds cheered at the nimble Model A's ascent to the top of the stairs, and soon brave imitators copied the feat on the steps of their own local courthouse steps, often to the dismay of the local constable.

The one-cylinder's next conquest was organized racing. At least one Model A Cadillac recorded a win in organized racing around 1903, most likely with a stripped

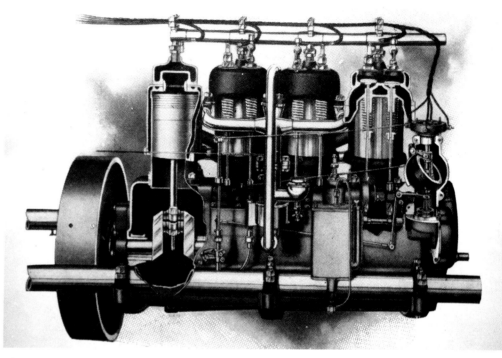

This cut-away shows the 30-horsepower Model H four-cylinder engine used between 1906 and 1908. (Cadillac Historical Collection)

Reassembled and ready for action: Three 1908 Cadillacs stop for a photo before they begin their 500-mile test at top speed to prove the interchangeability of their parts. (GM Media Archives)

body that helped it exceed the car's claimed top speed of 30 mph fully dressed. Soon, other race car drivers found potential in the Cadillac chassis and raced them wherever they could.

Only five years later, the skeptical Royal Automobile Club put Cadillac ingenuity and performance to the ultimate test when it completely disassembled three complete Cadillacs, mixed their components, and reassembled the cars for a brisk 500-mile spin around the Brooklands Motordrome in London, England.

The one-cylinder Cadillac performed effortlessly and with a remarkable average speed of 34 mph.

Speed hounds dreamed of what they could do with the 70-horsepower eight-cylinder Cadillac of 1915, and E. G. "Canonball" Baker and W. F. Strum made the dream a reality when they embraced the power of the V-8 for a cross-country journey. Driving a 1916 Cadillac roadster, the pair sliced nearly four days off the previous Los Angeles-to-New York record time, which had been held by a Stutz Bearcat. In a little more than a week, the pair scaled mountains, blasted through the plains, and bounced through 3,741 miles of America's rough roads. The next week, another daring driver, T. J. Beaudet, bested the record time for the 450 mile-plus journey between Los Angeles and San Francisco. By driving through the night, Beaudet was able to beat the

Dealers were encouraged to save durable V-8 Cadillac chassis that may have been wrecked and convert them to wrecker use. This helped promote the idea that Cadillac chassis were superior and durable. This beautifully built 1927 Cadillac service car is shown leaving a dealership on its way to a call. (GM Media Archives)

This stripped chassis awaits reassembly by Royal Automobile Club mechanics for the group's standardization of parts test on the 1908 one-cylinder Cadillac. (GM Media Archives)

The head of Cadillac's experimental staff, Willard "Big Bill" Rader, poses with the LaSalle and the driver who accompanied him on the durability run, dirt track racer Gus Bell. (GM Media Archives)

fastest train connecting the two cities, a common method of measuring a car's performance at the time, by averaging 48 mph.

The next big step was the introduction of the V-8-powered LaSalle in 1927. To prove its prowess, a stripped down 75-horsepower LaSalle Series 303 roadster piloted by Cadillac experimental driver Willard "Big Bill" Rader, accompanied by famous dirt track racer Gus Bell, thundered around the General Motors Proving Grounds for 10 straight hours at an average speed of 95.3 mph. Members of the media were on hand to witness the

The official car of the Indianapolis 500 was this V-16 dual-cowl phaeton, Cadillac's new industry-shaking sensation. The car was assigned to Indianapolis Motor Speedway president Colonel E.V. Knickerbocker. Meanwhile, a white 1931 V-12 roadster assumed pace car duties. (Old Cars Weekly archives)

To prove the new 1927 LaSalle's prowess, a Series 303 roadster shed its extraneous fenders, windshield, and headlights for a run before media members at the Milford Proving Grounds. The car averaged 95.3 mph, not far off the top speed of Indy cars of the day. Here, the LaSalle passes the pits during the 950-mile durability test. (GM Media Archives)

Right: *LaSalle led the Indianapolis 500 pack for its second time in 1934 with this convertible coupe. The sporty blue LaSalle was piloted by Bill Rader, but it wasn't powered by a Cadillac engine. For the first time in the marque's history, Cadillac used an engine from another General Motors division. All LaSalles were powered by a 240-cid straight eight built by Oldsmobile to Cadillac standards. (Old Cars Weekly archives)*

Charles F. Kettering poses with the first-generation V-16 engine. (GM Media Archives)

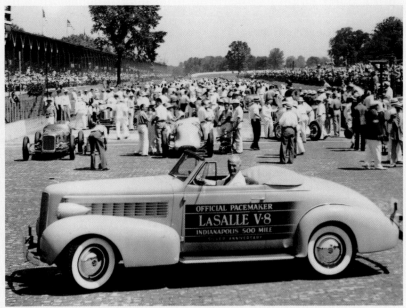

Cadillacs and LaSalles have spread their tread on the hallowed race surface at the Indianapolis Motor Speedway several times over the years. By 1937, LaSalle was already pacing its third race—an amazing honor, especially since the car was a youthful 10 years old at the time. Former race car driver Ralph DePalma is shown posing with the pace car he drove in the 1937 Indianapolis 500.

spectacular accomplishment and document the fenderless LaSalle's durability. Durability may have been the point Cadillac wanted to demonstrate, but it was the car's speed that impressed the press. At 95.3 mph, the LaSalle was only 2 mph slower than the winner of that year's Indianapolis 500, and it had endured twice the distance!

The LaSalle's combination of beauty and speed scored big with buyers, and it became clear Cadillac had another hit by combining quality and performance into a handsome package. But Cadillac wasn't done. A secret program to develop a 16-cylinder Cadillac had been in the works for several years, and its announcement at the end of 1929 jolted the industry. Beautifully styled inside and out, the overhead-valve V-16 featured hydraulic valve silencers for quiet operation, but it deceptively hid 165 horsepower beneath its polished aluminum and luminous chrome exterior. Even when placed in a large, palatial limousine, the V-16 could roar a Fleetwood-bodied model to speeds in excess of 80 mph. When the engine went into a racy Fleetwood roadster, the speedometer of a V-16 could easily muscle past the 100-mph mark.

A second dignified monster appeared in 1931 when the equally beautiful V-12 engine merged into Cadillac's catalog. Also known for its smooth and quiet operation, the 368-cid V-12 gained respect for its awesome performance.

A Cadillac sedan eats up the concrete at the Milford Proving Grounds test track. (GM Media Archives)

The mostly stock 1950 Cadillac Series 61 coupe entered by Briggs Cunningham pits at the 1950 24 Hours of Le Mans race. The banners above the pits indicate the Cadillac-powered Allard was in an adjacent pit. (Cadillac Historical Collection)

Cadillac quickly got to work proving the 135-horsepower V-12 was no slouch. And there was no better place than the race track. A brilliant white V-12 roadster was assigned pace car duties at the 1931 Indianapolis 500 race, and it ate up the track at a commanding and record-breaking 100 mph under the charge of Rader. The publicity worked, and V-12 sales quickly surpassed the impressive figures earned by the 1930 V-16 models.

Cunningham's Series 61 coupe thunders through a turn at the 1950 24 Hours of Le Mans race in this photo. The car finished a respectable 10th overall. (Cadillac Historical Collection)

The battle-scarred number 127 1954 Cadillac coupe driven by Colorado racer Keith Andrews and co-piloted by Blue Plemond placed third in the Large Stock Class and 11th overall at the 1954 La Carrera Panamericana race that year. A second Cadillac, driven by Edward A. Stringer and co-piloted by Truman C. Wood, placed 14th overall. (GM Media Archives)

Bearing signs of road rash on its front fender, the roll bar-equipped 1954 Cadillac coupe driven by Keith Andrews returned to the Clark Street plant for this photo opportunity. The Cadillac posted the fastest top speed in its class but, despite gaining on the early lead set by Ray Crawford in a 1954 Lincoln Capri, the Cadillac was unable to get to the finish line first. Andrews' car placed a respectable third in the Large Stock Class and 11th overall. (GM Media Archives)

The promising might of the V-12s and V-16s didn't go unnoticed by the hot rodding community. By dumping either of Cadillac's multi-cylinder engines into a small, light Ford roadster or a belly tank race car, a driver had an instant hot rod that could eat up earth in California's salt flats or scorch pavement in stop sign sprints on city streets. Due to their high cost and relative rarity, coupled with the lack of aftermarket hop-up goodies, the engines saw limited use. But those that did find their way into highboy Model A's and channeled Deuce roadsters provided plenty of thrills.

The strong LaSalle transmission found more use in the hot rodding community. Post-World War II performance-part businesses thrived on producing adaptors that coupled the LaSalle transmission to an engine from another manufacturer. Rodders usually scrapped the gears for first and reverse to lighten up the transmission even further.

The overhead-valve V-12s and V-16s disappeared after the 1937 model year, and most suspected it was the end to Cadillac's grand experiment with the multi-cylinder power plants. But Cadillac had another surprise for its doubters with the launch of an entirely new V-16 series. New bodies and a fresh flathead V-16 became available in 1938, but the engines lacked the exterior flash of its

Any mother could cart her daughter off to pres-chool quickly with Cadillac's standard 250-horsepower, 331-cid V-8. When packing the optional 270-horsepower, dual-carbureted Eldorado engine, the '55 Cadillac became a factory-issued hot rod.

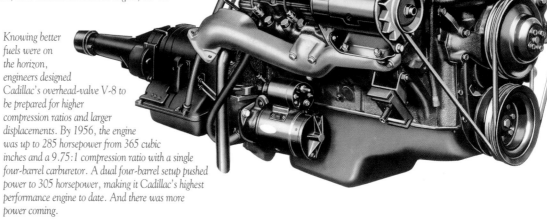

beautifully designed overhead-valve predecessor. The engine's appearance was likely of little concern because it sat so low in the engine compartment of the broader and more massive 1938 Series 90 Cadillacs. Consequently, the models have never achieved the same aura of the first series V-16 models.

Cadillac set fire to the world of performance when it revisited overhead-valve engine design in the late 1940s. This time the surprise was a 90-degree, overhead-valve V-8. Light in weight and efficient in operation, the relatively small 331-cid engine boasted 160 horsepower.

Doubts about the engine's potential lingered through the overhead-valve's inaugural year, but racing sportsman Briggs Swift Cunningham laid them all to rest with his successful Cadillac entries at the 1950 Le Mans 24-Hour ace. The first Cadillac, a stripped

Knowing better fuels were on the horizon, engineers designed Cadillac's overhead-valve V-8 to be prepared for higher compression ratios and larger displacements. By 1956, the engine was up to 285 horsepower from 365 cubic inches and a 9.75:1 compression ratio with a single four-barrel carburetor. A dual four-barrel setup pushed power to 305 horsepower, making it Cadillac's highest performance engine to date. And there was more power coming.

Luxury and performance harmonized in the 1957 Cadillac Eldorado Seville coupe. Leather-and-fine cloth upholstery and a roof covering brought luxury, and a dual-carbureted, 300-horsepower V-8 engine throbbed under the hood. (GM Media Archives)

The dual four-barrel-carbureted, 300-horsepower V-8 in this 1957 Eldorado Brougham undergoes performance testing at General Motors' desert proving grounds in Mesa, Arizona. (GM Media Archives)

Series 61 coupe with Cadillac's shortest wheelbase, went into the race with minor mechanical improvements for added safety and reliability and no changes to its exterior. A new body was crafted for the second Series 61 coupe chassis by nearby Grumman Aircraft Corporation's metal fabricators and was quickly dubbed "Le Monstre" by the French press for its appalling appearance. Cunningham was permitted a few mechanical changes to Le Monstre's otherwise stock chassis—the most notable was a five-carburetor manifold and prototype 2.9:1 rear axle gears designed by Ed Cole. Cunningham's Frick-Tappet Motors installed the parts and prepared both three-speed, manual transmission cars for competition.

Even with a more aerodynamic body, Le Monstre could not beat its stock-bodied sibling, but its unusual body wasn't the sole source of blame. A nasty slide into a sand bank in Mulsanne set Briggs scooping sand to free the car and cost him 30 minutes, and the Grumman-bodied car lacked speed when pulling out of turns in the course. The stock-bodied coupe didn't enjoy much better luck. At the start of the race, the drivers found the doors locked, sending them scurrying for the keys. Despite the obstacles, the Cadillacs performed well. The coupe finished 10th overall with Le Monstre right behind in 11th. Crowds cheered and a new respect was born. A lightweight, Cadillac-powered Allard J-2 finished in third place overall, proving that Cadillac power was right at home on the track.

Cadillac's trials at Le Mans impressed the world and impacted the way large American cars were viewed. More importantly, the success directed Americans to look at Cadillac as a performance innovator with a track record to back it up.

Cadillac's famous batwing-shaped air cleaner signaled the engine was topped by a multi-carbureted engine, which Cadillac referred to as the "Q" engine. The batwing air cleaner on this engine hides the dual-carburetor setup standard on 1957 Cadillac Eldorados or the triple-carburetor setup found on 1958 Eldorados. The multi-carbureted "Q" engines were optional on other Cadillacs.

The horsepower war was officially on. Weekend racers began taking their Cadillacs to American race tracks, and many found the only competitors in their class to be overhead-valve-packing Rocket 88 Oldsmobiles. Cadillac kept up with the race through the 1950s with its dual- and triple-carbureted Eldorado engines and increased compression ratios. By 1955, any Cadillac could be powered by the 331-cid, 270-horsepower Eldorado engine that quenched its thirst through a pair of four-barrel carburetors. Displacement was upped to 365 cubic inches for 1956, and again, a dual four-barrel carburetor Eldorado engine was available. The engines had a higher 9.75:1 compression ratio and horsepower grew to 285. The final multi-carbureted Cadillac, the 1960 model,

The massive and angry-looking front of this 1959 Cadillac six-window sedan presumably struck fear into the hearts of fellow drivers as it crossed through the dirt-packed center of the figure eight at Ascot Speedway in Gardena, California, when it was raced there in the late 1960s or early 1970s. Such cars were rarely raced because of their length and the increased danger they posed when crossing through the "x" at figure eight tracks. (Ron Kowalke collection)

Although this 1941 Cadillac Sedanette, entered by Johnny Dietz Racing, didn't win the race, this photo shows it put up a formidable battle against the winner, the number 5 car driven by Paul Bjork following closely behind. The Johnny Dietz Racing team's entry wasn't sanctioned by Cadillac in this 1948 Milwaukee Mile stock car race, but its powerful flathead engine and its slick roof design made the Sedanette a formidable machine. (Armin Krueger photo; Greenfield Gallery collection)

strutted a 345-horsepower rating for the triple-carbureted 390-cid Eldorado engine. After 1960, Cadillac would rely on a single four-barrel carburetor to do the breathing and gas-sipping duties.

Hot rodders again found potential in the 90-degree, overhead-valve Cadillac engine, just as they had with the engine's overhead-valve V-16 forefather, and more than a few Cadillac engines found themselves behind the radiator of a 20-year-old jalopy. Since a new Cadillac was out of their price range, American youths did the next best thing and planted a powerful Cadillac engine in their old Ford or Chevrolet body. This time, hot rodders found support through aftermarket companies. Manufacturers like Edelbrock and Moon Equipment offered aluminum valve covers and valley pan covers. Some even built multi-carburetor manifolds for the Cadillac engine. One of the most fabulous uses of the Cadillac power plant was in the "Emperor," a heavily chromed and modified Model A roadster that won the 1960 Oakland Roadster Show. Owned by Chuck Krikorian, the "Emperor" was built in the shop of famous custom car builder George Barris. The showcase of this hot rod was its exposed Cadillac engine topped by six Stromberg carburetors on a fully chromed chassis.

By the early to mid 1960s, manufacturers began following the lead set by hot rodders and started putting powerful engines in their now-diversified lineups for serious race duty. Cadillac began to focus more on increased comfort and

Cadillac's performance numbers rose through the 1950s, thanks to increased compression ratios and cylinder boring on the original 90-degree, overhead-valve 331-cid engine that debuted in 1949. By 1959, the overhead-valve engine displaced 390 cubic inches and had a standard 325-horsepower rating when equipped with the single four-barrel carburetor. (GM Media Archives)

convenience in its cars without sacrificing power. No engine whispering beneath the crested hood of a Caddy put out any less than 325 horsepower through the 1960s. Cadillac engineers even redesigned the V-8 in 1963 to be as powerful as its 325-horsepower, 390-cid 1962 predecessor, but with less external size and weight. The new V-8 was built for further growth and increased power, and was bored up to 429 cubic inches and 340 horsepower by 1967, its final year.

With the horsepower race raging on in Detroit and the "more cubes, more power" axiom being truer than ever, Cadillac ensured it would maintain the lead on engine displacement with a new 472-cubic inch V-8 in 1968. The Goliath engine was powerful, but it was engineered with driver comfort and efficiency in mind—two doctrines that were the driving force in Cadillac philosophy throughout the 1960s. Integrated into the new engine was an integral distribution system for Cadillac's pollution-control system and air conditioning compressor mounts, a first for any manufacturer. Even with more accessories fastened to the engine, Cadillac was able to fashion a smaller and simplified power plant that required few components while putting out an arresting 375 horsepower.

Not content with that horsepower rating, Cadillac upped the ante with a 500-cid engine planted between every 1970 Eldorado's front fenders. The engine produced an awesome 400 horsepower with an astonishing 550 lbs.-ft. of torque, allowing the luxury coupe to assault any asphalt surface with its front tires all day long. Calais and deVille models would have to wait until 1975 before they would be gifted with the 500-cid V-8, the world's largest mass-produced engine. Unfortunately, emissions restrictions and a reduced compression choked the thunderous 500-cid engine down to a dismal 190 horsepower.

Through the 1970s and 1980s, horsepower ratings would become less critical throughout the industry as concerns over fuel economy rose. Cadillac delivered the best of both worlds with the 425-cid V-8 offered in 1977 models. After testing 110 experimental engine designs, the 425-cid V-8 was selected for its healthy 180 horsepower and its relatively small size and lightweight construction. Cadillac customers were awarded with the marque's hallmark smooth performance, but now with greater fuel economy. The new smaller and

The dual exhaust system was gone, as was the optional multi-carbureted engine option, but Cadillac continued to offer performance in its luxury products. This airy 1961 Coupe deVille with a bubble-top greenhouse used the only engine available—the 325-horsepower, 390-cid V-8 engine carried over from 1960. Since the 1961 Cadillac was several inches shorter and more than 100 lbs. lighter than its predecessor, the 390-cid power plant had less car to pull from a stop light. (GM Media Archives)

Even four-doors were tested for performance with varying assaults on their mechanical components. In this photo, the cornering prowess on a 1965 Cadillac sedan undergoes testing on a rough surface. (GM Media Archives)

Emergency personnel trusted the power of the 472-cid V-8 in the 1970 Cadillac commercial chassis. This factory photo was staged to show the duties this Hess and Eisenhardt ambulance would experience in the field. (GM Media Archives)

In the third production year of the famous 500-cid V-8, Cadillac, like all other automakers, began expressing the horsepower rating in both net and gross figures. Due to constricting pollution-control requirements in the early 1970s, the 500-cid V-8 engine pumped out 365 gross horsepower and 235 net horsepower by 1972, the year this Fleetwood Eldorado was built. The rating was down from a high of 400 net horsepower in 1970, the first year the 500-cid engine was installed in the Eldorado line. (GM Media Archives)

The 1985 Eldorado Touring Coupe was Cadillac's attack on the European sports cars from Mercedes and BMW in the 1980s and cost $1,975 more than a base Eldorado. (GM Media Archives)

lighter 1977 Cadillac body could also be fit with electronic fuel injection, which upped horsepower to 195 units. The early 1980s marked a low in Cadillac performance. Large cars with small horsepower figures plagued the automaker's performance image. Of no help was the troublesome V-8-6-4

Acceleration became a priority in Cadillac by the late 1980s, and was addressed with a new 4.5-Liter V-8 that outperformed comparable Cadillacs of the previous decade. (GM Media Archives)

With the Northstar V-8 under the hood, the 2001 Cadillac Seville is one hot performer. (GM Media Archives)

Cadillac started to regain the respect of the industry when it unveiled the Northstar V-8 engine in 1993. By 2001, the Northstar engine delivered 275 horsepower in luxury-oriented Cadillacs and 300 horsepower in the sportier Eldorado Touring Coupes and Seville Touring Sedans. (GM Media Archives)

The 1993 model year marked the only time the Allante' was available with the Northstar engine. As a result, it is the most desired model year.

engine that featured a computer to shut down cylinders to accommodate maximum fuel efficiency in a variety of conditions. The lethargic 4.1-liter V-8 and a like-sized V-6 engine further tarnished Cadillac's performance image in the early 1980s. It would take years to repair the damage and a very special automobile to convince the public that performance was a language still spoken by Cadillac engineers. And what better way than to convince buyers than through an Italian-built, two-seat convertible.

The new-for-1987 Allanté took the font-wheel-drive-arranged 4.1-liter engine and specially tuned it, then added an aluminum oil pan and magnesium rocker arm covers. Power increased with the addition of a 4.5-

The CTS is truly a driver's car built for the automobile enthusiast who expects the drive to work to be more than a commute. (Cadillac Historical Collection)

liter V-8 in 1989, courtesy of low-restriction exhaust manifolds and a better-flowing air cleaner. The Allanté posted 0 to 60-mph times just over the eight-second mark and a top speed of 135 mph. Peppy-performing Fleetwoods, Sevilles, and both deVille models benefited from the larger engine the previous year.

Displacement increases were accompanied by higher horsepower input at the start of the 1990s with a 4.9-liter engine, but it is the Northstar engine that has been the star behind Cadillac's performance quest since 1993. When the Northstar was installed in the flagship Seville sedan, Cadillac claimed horsepower was increased 45 percent over the previous year's larger, 4.9-liter engine. The 4.6-liter pounded out 295 horsepower and spun the Seville Touring Sedan up to a maximum speed of 150 mph. The Eldorado Sport Coupe, Eldorado Touring Coupe, and Allanté also benefited from the 32-valve, four-cam powerhouse in the Northstar's inaugural year.

With the Northstar available to all Cadillac's front-wheel-drive cars in 1994, the company had firmly established itself as a performance contender in the luxury field. New, power-starved buyers were turning to Cadillac.

Aggressive performance continues into the new millennium and, again, the Northstar is lighting Cadillac's path. Current Cadillac offerings provide a minimum of 275 horsepower in the Seville and deVille lines, and the rocketship deVille DTS spits out 300 horsepower for corner-biting pleasure. Squeezing the most power out of the Northstar is the 2004 XLR, a fresh two-seat retractable-top convertible that cranks out 320 horsepower.

Cadillac returned to the 24 Hours of Le Mans endurance race with four race cars in 2000. Based on the Riley & Scott chassis, each LMP (Le Mans Prototype) was fitted with a twin-turbocharged, intercooled 4.0-liter Northstar V-8 engine. (Cadillac Historical Collection)

Cadillac encountered some problems in its 2000 Le Mans program, but made several improvements to the chassis and engine for a better showing in 2001. GM Racing also changed the race staff and contracted renowned race manager Jeff Hazell, designer Nigel Stroud, and race driver/commercial director Wayne Taylor to join the Team Cadillac program. (Cadillac Historical Collection)

Tempting Cadillac enthusiasts was Cadillac's Sixteen show car, introduced in 2003. The hyper-luxurious show stopper revived the exciting V-16 engine with a beautifully styled exterior matching the exterior looks of the original of 1930, but now the horsepower rating was up to 1,000. (GM Media Archives)

At the Spring 2003 New York Auto Show, GM executive Jim Taylor told reporters, "Cadillac is going through a renaissance in two directions, both product and image. To show that real change is taking place and to change old perceptions of our cars, we needed to jolt people into realizing something was going on. We did that with a fashion statement with the new look of the CTS."

The jolt went beyond the looks of the V-6-equipped 2003 Cadillac CTS. With the availability of the CTS V-Series in 2004, gutsy Cadillac drivers can experience a head-snapping 400-horsepower, V-8. The GM-built 5.7-liter LS6

engine shared with the Z06 Corvette will be the showcase of the aggressive-handling sport package that is expected to launch the mid-size sedan from a standstill to 60 mph in a miniscule 4.6 seconds. All this will be accomplished through a six-speed manual transmission—the first driver-shifted transmission since 1950.

Sunday drivers, get out of the way. Cadillac is coming. And fast.

Luxury

Technology. Comfort. Performance. These are all luxuries a Cadillac owner expects and receives in a new Cadillac, but they weren't immediately available in any car. It was a long evolutionary process that led to the computer-aided controls and the creature comforts found in today's Cadillacs.

In early motoring, simple closed-body options and a self-starting system were uncommon luxuries available to Cadillac customers, and refinements that engineered the Cadillac engine into one of the industry's smoothest power plants gave Cadillac an edge on luxury.

100 Years

Quality built into Cadillac's bodies added to the luxury, and a 1920 advertisement from the *Saturday Evening Post* quoting *The Motor-The National Motor Car Journal of Britain*, read: "The workmanship and finish on the Cadillac are equal to anything extant, whether it be a product of Europe or America."

With fine mohair fabrics and leathers available, a Cadillac interior could be trimmed as elegantly as its exterior through the 1920s. Leather tops, chrome wire wheels, and dual side mounts were available on both Cadillac and LaSalle models in the late 1920s. The company even offered a catalog of semi-custom bodies built by outside firms that could be tailored to meet the demands of an owner.

With the introduction of the mighty V-16 Cadillac of 1930, motorists were about to experience an all-new attention to luxury from Cadillac. A plethora of semi-custom bodies in a choice of styles allowed customers to select such details as straight or curved rocker sills, and windshield configuration.

In a brochure for the V-16, Cadillac touted, "The bodies are of many types, custom built and elaborately finished, and all highly individualized. Personal preference as in styling and colors can be fully expressed. The finish of panels, upholstery, fabrics, trim and other factors of style and beauty may be blended into distinctive expressions of individuality. Even major features of styling may be adapted to the individual taste."

Both Cadillacs and LaSalles benefit from elegant chrome treatments, and their bodies grew more streamlined through the early 1930s. Additional driving comfort came with Cadillac's introduction of knee-action shocks in 1934. The following year, Cadillacs received a road-stabilizing feature that reduced body roll during turns.

Very formal and personal, Cadillac's V-16 four-passenger coupe used a long 154-inch wheelbase that emphasized the car's long hood and rear deck. (GM Media Archives)

Under the breathtaking exterior of Dave Lindsay's 1930 Fleetwood-bodied all-weather phaeton lies a V-16 of equally stunning beauty and performance. This car's Owen Nacker-designed V-16 was the first engine to see a designer's touch with hidden wires and hoses and a beautiful mix of enamel paint, polished aluminum, and porcelain. (Angelo Van Bogart photo)

One of the benefits of owning a Cadillac in the 1930s was the company's residential service program. A Cadillac service employee drove out to the Cadillac owner's home by motorcycle, then hooked the motorcycle to the back of the car and drove it to the dealership for service. The Cadillac could also be returned to the owner in the same manner, providing unmatched convenience. This driver is from the Detroit Branch of the Cadillac Motor Car Company. (GM Media Archives)

A well-dressed member of the Cadillac residential service program returns with a sedan for service at a Cadillac-LaSalle garage. Note the manner in which the motorcycle is attached to the back of the car. (GM Media Archives)

Luxury began with the V-8 Cadillacs and ended with the V-16s in 1931. Richard A. Esposito's V-8-powered Series 355-A convertible coupe shares many of its styling features, most notably in the grille area, with the more expensive V-16 and new-for-the-year V-12 models.

Streamlining through rounder body lines and skirted fenders, coupled with a light reduction of exterior brightwork, gave Cadillac and LaSalle models a new understated, yet classy, look. One of the greatest benefactors of this look was the new-for-1938 Sixty Special. Its large pontoon fenders, Art Deco horizontally ribbed grille, and classic formal roof exuded a new kind of Cadillac luxury. Inviting curved window frames offered a lightness to the cabin and, at slightly more than $2,000, it was attractively priced.

Also new in 1938 was the optional "Sunshine Turret Top Roof," which was essentially a retractable sunroof that afforded a view of the sky by sliding the panel toward the back of the car. Such a feature was usually

Even the chauffeur of Cadillac's 1931 V-16 Transformable Town Cabriolet was surrounded with fine grain leather upholstery and door panels. Luxury came at a price, however; this V-16 model carried a shocking $8,750 price tag.

The profile of this Fleetwood Imperial Cabriolet body exudes luxury. The contrasting roof covering, the wheels discs, and the rounded edges of the chrome window frames are evident on this 1932 Cadillac V-16 model built for a Mr. Klingler, according to records. Four of these cars were apparently built. (GM Media Archives)

limited to custom-built automobiles, but Cadillac and LaSalle made it optional on their production cars. Though it was perfect for watching the stars on a cool spring night or feeling the sun on a warm summer

Cadillac backed up its attack on the luxury market with the V-12 in 1931, one year after the introduction of the V-16. The move shocked the automotive world, just as the V-16 introduction had one year earlier. Dave Lindsay's V-12 roadster carries a semi-custom Fleetwood body designed by Harley Earl and Ernest Schebera. (Angelo Van Bogart photo)

The entry point to Cadillac luxury in 1937 was the Series 60, which included a sedan, coupe, convertible coupe, and convertible sedan models. This 1937 Series 60 coupe, owned by John E. Brewer, was originally priced at $1,665, factory delivered and before options.

A 1940 Cadillac Sixty Special sedan demonstrates its Sunshine Turret Top Roof. The predecessor to the sunroof was ahead of its time, and it would take more than 30 years for the innovation to become popular. (GM Media Archives)

Even Cadillac part and accessory packages were artfully designed to convey luxury. (Kris Kandler/Bob Best photo)

day, few buyers enjoyed the romantic feature, and only 1,500 were installed on Cadillacs and LaSalles before the option was discontinued at the end of 1941.

Keeping a Cadillac cool was made easier with the introduction of air conditioning in 1941, though only 300 cars were equipped with the feature. Using the system was difficult, and to turn it on or off a driver had to install or remove a belt from the engine. When installed, the belt ran the air conditioner constantly. To disconnect the system, a driver had to shut the car off and remove the belt. The compartment-cooling option was a quick answer to Packard's availability of the system as early as 1939, and it wasn't until after the war that the system became more convenient to operate.

After matching Packard's luxury feature with its own air-conditioning system in 1941, Cadillac one-upped its rival with the addition of a fully automatic transmission—the Hydra-Matic. Gone forever was the need to shift gears manually, and 30 percent of 1941 Cadillac buyers chose to eliminate the task by selecting the Hydra-Matic. One decade later, Cadillac eliminated its manual transmissions altogether.

Cadillac was ready to raise the level of luxury in its offerings as the demand for new cars trailed off in the postwar period. Concept models at GM's Transportation Unlimited show in New York displayed features like specially upholstered broadcloth and leather interiors, silver-plated interior

hardware, and cowhide interior in the Cadillac convertible, hardtop coupe, and Sixty Special show cars. At the 1950 Mid-Century Motorama held at New York's Waldorf-Astoria Hotel, Cadillac followed up its 1949 show cars with a new 1950 Series 62 convertible. With a leopard pelt-trimmed interior and gold plating throughout, the bright yellow car, dubbed the "Debutante," was a show-stealing sight, but it would soon be upstaged.

A new starlet hit the stage in 1952 in the form of a customized Cadillac Series 62 convertible sporting a wrap-around windshield and a flush-mounted top boot cover. Bestowed with the name "Eldorado," Spanish for "the golden one," the show car predicted a new model for the 1953 model year that would be available to anyone willing to swallow the car's weighty $7,750 price tag. Cadillac's golden one showed a clear departure from the formal luxury of its Sixty Special and Series Seventy Five stable mates by making its amenities more intimate. A wraparound windshield, cut-down doors, and a flush top boot cover combined sporty athleticism with Cadillac opulence, and gave the Cadillac name an entirely new and debonair attitude.

Only 532 Eldorados were built in the first production year, but the car's flair provided additional status to the Cadillac nameplate that couldn't be ignored. Few people were lucky enough to experience an Eldorado in person, but they had their chance on television and in newspapers when President Dwight D. Eisenhower waved to his people from the backseat of a flag-toting Eldorado in his January 1953 inaugural parade.

The upscale Broadmoor Hotel in Colorado Springs, Colorado, chose luxurious Hess and Eisenhardt-built Cadillacs to chauffeur vacationing guests up and down Pike's Peak and the red rock gardens. This 1955 Cadillac sightseeing coach was one of a long line of Cadillacs used by the hotel, and it certainly wasn't the last. (GM Media Archives)

The visible roof panels on top of the 1955 Cadillacs used by the Broadmoor Hotel in Colorado Springs, Colorado, for transporting guests earned the Hess and Eisenhardt-built Cadillacs the name "Sky View." (GM Media Archives)

A luxurious 1957 Cadillac Fleetwood Sixty Special receives a buffing for GM's famous lacquer shine before heading off the Clark Street assembly line. (GM Media Archives)

The new Seville and Sedan deVille models were the newest additions to Cadillac's lineup and bowed October 24, 1955, almost one month before the rest of the 1956 models made it to showrooms. This 1956 Seville sports the rich-looking Vicodec roof covering. (GM Media Archives)

The Eldorado returned for the 1954 model year with sheet metal that was far less distinct than it had been the previous year, but with a reduced price ($5,738) that made it more attainable. Special touches included ribbed chrome fender trim, a fiberglass boot cover, and an especially luxurious interior.

The direction of Eldorado and its role in the Cadillac line became clear when the shark-finned 1955 Eldorados swam into showrooms. Aggressive fin styling reserved only for the Eldorado was matched by an equally aggressive power plant that defined the model as a luxury sport car with tip-of-the-sword styling. Inside, the luxury continued with chromed steering column covers and a unique bullet-shaped chrome horn button. Even the inviting interior was fit with an Eldorado-only leather pattern to complete the ultimate luxury package.

A vinyl roof covering, leather interior, chrome appointments inside and out, optional air conditioning, and the convenient power of dual four-barrel carburetors made the 1956 Seville Cadillac's premier luxury coupe offering for the year, even beating out the posh Coupe deVille of the same year. (Ed Hughes photo)

The ultimate luxury car to come from any automaker in the 1950s was the Eldorado Brougham. Pillarless doors without a center post between the doors, a brushed stainless-steel roof, and a compact, elegant exterior were hallmarks of the ultra-luxury Cadillac. The luxury continued inside with mouton or high-pile Karakul carpet, memory seating, and a matched set of vanities and party accoutrements in the glove compartment and rear armrest.

Cadillac would honor the Eldorado nameplate with multi-carbureted, high-performance engines through 1960, but the unique styling features and upgraded interior appointments would be a hallmark through the model's run as a rear-wheel-drive automobile in 1966.

The addition of a luxury sport coupe Seville model to the Eldorado line in 1956 reflected Cadillac's commitment to the personal luxury automobile, but even the details that made the Seville hardtop coupe and Biarritz convertible Eldorados couldn't compare to Cadillac's ultimate nod to the luxury genre—the 1957 Cadillac Eldorado Brougham. Much more than a four-door Eldorado, the Brougham featured unique styling that predicted the widespread use of the quad-headlight system and the sleek, low lines that would become the industry

The chauffeur of a 1959 Cadillac Fleetwood 75 was treated to leather upholstery in a variety of colors complementing the Bedford cord upholstery in the rear compartment. (GM Media Archives)

Cadillac turned down the Buick Riviera design in the early 1960s because it had this personal luxury coupe, the 1967 Fleetwood Eldorado, in mind since the late 1950s. A close-coupled engine compartment eased between a long hood and a short rear deck offered a new kind of intimacy in the Cadillac lineup. (GM Media Archives)

Many Cadillac customers yearned for the family-hauling abilities of a station wagon to be coupled with the luxury of a Cadillac, but they couldn't find what they were looking for on dealers' lots. Custom body makers solved the dilemma by creating a Cadillac-based station wagon for a customer, but at considerable cost. (GM Media Archives)

Cadillac continued to offer the luxurious and stately Fleetwood Sixty Special in 1962. Any fedora-capped businessman could confidently exit this sedan with pride. (GM Media Archives)

standard by the end of the 1950s.

Truly the tuxedo of Cadillac's 1957 lineup, the Brougham featured a stainless-steel roof with a streak pattern matching a gentleman's Brylcream-drenched pompadour, and Dagmars large enough to elbow off any force in front of it, including Lincoln's Continental Mark II, the Brougham's only competition.

While a fine automobile in its own right, the Continental Mark II couldn't compare with the Brougham's ostentatious level of luxury, exemplified by the Cadillac's stratospheric $13,074 price tag. The Continental Mark II wasn't cheap, either, at $9,966.

For the equivalent of two Eldorado Biarritz models and some leftover change to go towards a Chevy, an Eldorado Brougham buyer bought more than a second set of doors. They bought ultimate expression in luxury motoring. Fine rugs, cutting edge-technology, and attention to detail were just a few of the items that made the Brougham the star of any parking lot.

Like a lady of fine taste, the Cadillac came with a matched set of accessories to prepare a driver and passenger for a state occasion or social outing. The rear armrest concealed a mirror, notepad and pencil, and a bottle of Arpège perfume extract. In the glove box hid a second mirror, a tissue dispenser, cigarette case, and six magnetized metallic tumblers that could be arranged on the opened glove box door.

And the ride of the Brougham was as smooth as its exterior. A revolutionary air suspension system replaced coil-and-spring arrangements, and an anti-dive control prevented the chrome Dagmars in the front bumper from pointing at the ground during braking maneuvers. Technology was matched inside with an ignition system that automatically started the car when it was placed in "park" or "neutral" with the key in the "on" position. The six-way power front seat catered to the driver and remembered his favorite position, to which it could be returned at any time.

A power sunroof accompanied by an elk-grain padded vinyl roof signified a 1972 Cadillac Fleetwood Eldorado owner had sprung for the Custom Cabriolet option. (GM Media Archives)

It didn't get more luxurious than the Fleetwood Sixty Special Brougham in 1972. A choice of upholsteries included Sierra grain leathers, Matador cloths, Minuet fabrics, or the posh-feeling Medici crushed velour. Adding further luxury was the Dual Comfort front seats and individual rear seat reading lamps. (GM Media Archives)

Combinations of high-grade leathers and fine materials, accented by dashes of chrome and stainless trim, typified the interiors of Cadillac's luxurious 1960s models. An emphasis on convenience options to maximize the motoring experience also became apparent as Cadillac took advantage of new technologies. Cruise control, optional first in late-1950s Cadillacs, grew in popularity.

Conveniences found in the finest homes soon found their way into the chrome-trimmed driver command centers of 1960s Cadillacs—the most famous being the Comfort Control system. Beginning in 1964, Cadillacs could be ordered with a system that allowed the driver to select a cabin temperature, and the

Robert Newbrough's 1978 Eldorado Biarritz sports such luxury features as an Elk grain padded vinyl top, electric level control, automatic climate control, and cornering lights, among other features.

Only 704 first-generation Eldorado Broughams were sold during its two-year run, but it convinced America of Cadillac's supremacy as the country's luxury leader. Cadillac continued the program two more years, in 1959 and 1960, but the cars lost some of their distinctive features, most notably the stainless-steel roof. Built by Pinin Farina in Turin, Italy, the restyled 1959 and 1960 Broughams didn't look much different from production Cadillacs to the casual observer, but

Luxury continued inside the 1978 Eldorado Biarritz with Sierra grain leather contoured pillow-style seats, a vanity mirror, and even a color-keyed litter container.

The Custom Phaeton option on the 1979 Cadillac Sedan deVille had a convertible-style roof covering that was similar to the original Custom Phaeton top of the 1920s, right down to the stitching and small, convertible-style back window. (GM Media Archives)

they shared no body panels with the production Cadillacs of the same years. More sedately styled, the Brougham forged on with fewer technological innovations, and coupled with some subtle differences between it and the lesser-priced Cadillac models, did not sell well. Still commanding an extremely high price tag of $13,074, only 99 Broughams were sold in 1959 and 101 in 1960.

The Brougham exercise was a money-losing proposition for Cadillac, but it exemplified the image of Cadillac luxury. It would not be repeated, though many features in the Broughams found their way into the rest of the Cadillac lineup, including the air suspension and memory seat, which are still found on cars today.

Cadillac described the classically styled and skirted 1989 Fleetwood Sixty Special as a "luxuriously equipped up-level sedan with all-new styling… [and] a unique and sumptuous seating package trimmed in ultrasoft leather." (GM Media Archives)

Cadillac luxury could be found in the padded top and skirted fenders on the 1992 Cadillac Fleetwood coupe.

The Allanté's Nuance leather-trimmed bucket seats were orthopedically designed for optimum support and comfort.

To the surprise of the industry, Cadillac introduced an all-new Fleetwood Brougham in 1993 with a 5.7-liter, 185-horsepower V-8 engine that had enough power to pull an Airstream trailer.

heater or air conditioner would work to maintain that temperature through all seasons of the year. Further convenience came from the Twilight Sentinel, a device that turned a Cadillac's headlights on at dusk and off at dawn. When the engine was shut off, the headlights remained on for 90 seconds for driver safety.

In 1995, drivers could order an adjustable tilt and telescopic steering wheel that positioned the wheel in an infinite amount of positions for driver comfort. To further coddle the driver, a heated front seat option followed in 1966.

The personal luxury theme was revisited when Cadillac unleashed an all-new

Eldorado in 1967. A close-coupled passenger compartment sandwiched between a long hood and a short deck brought Cadillac into the muscle car era, but its design oozed Cadillac class with chrome-edge razor taillights and hidden headlights behind an egg-crate Cadillac grille. Front-wheel drive powered the wheels from the healthy 429-cid V-8. Highly popular with buyers, the Eldorado spawned a formula that would carry Cadillac luxury to coupe lovers for more than 30 years.

Couch-like comfort brought the Lazy Boy from the living room to the cabin of a Cadillac as seat designs enveloped the driver in plush leathers and cloth fabrics unavailable in lesser brands. Materials usually reserved for the interiors were increasingly being applied to the roofs of Cadillacs in the form of vinyl tops. The practice was common with leathers on the more prestigious Cadillacs of the 1930s and the exclusive Sevilles of the 1950s, but even entry-level Calais models were often outfitted with the luxurious-looking vinyl roof coverings by the late 1960s and early 1970s. By the 1980s, few Cadillacs could be found without the elegant touch.

Plush seat material, added lighting conveniences, and deep-pile carpets greeted privileged Fleetwood Brougham buyers who ordered the luxury model's new "Brougham d'Elegance" option in 1973. The option would bring similar luxuries to deVille models in 1974 and the rest of the Cadillac line through the 1980s.

Cadillac needed more than the interior luxury appointments of the d'Elegance package to compete with the growing number of imported luxury cars by

Even in 1993, the Allante's last year of availability, Cadillac continued to increase the luxury experience for drivers with new headlamp washers and heated outside rearview mirrors. New Northstar power that year made the Allanté a natural for pace duties at the Indianapolis 500 race, and it has been said that the Allanté was the only pace car at that point that did not require modifications to meet pacemaking performance requirements.

Trucks have evolved into more than furniture haulers; many people now expect them to be people haulers, as well. Cadillac brought luxury to the utilitarian field of trucks with its EXT in 2002. (Cadillac Historical Collection)

the mid 1970s, and it confronted the luxury market competition with the Seville in 1975. The entirely new model resurrected the luxury coupe nameplate Cadillac used from 1956-'60, but aside from its padded roof covering and numerous power controls, the Seville shared little with its predecessor. Outside, the Seville was shaped with crisp and angular European styling, but inside, the typical American luxuries abounded with fine fabrics and leathers, Cadillac's tilt-and-telescopic steering wheel, and air conditioning.

Seville helped trigger the computer craze in automobiles with its use of digital electronics for its trip computer. Only two years later, in 1977, integrated

Inside Automotive International Magazine awarded the 1998 Cadillac Seville its "Automotive Interior of the Year Award" based on its styling, safety features, and innovative use of materials. Cadillac designers Liz Wetzel and Dennis Little were responsible for the interior and exterior design of the restyled Seville. Upon accepting the award, Wetzel said, "Our goal was to create a passenger compartment that is both beautifully functional and tastefully luxurious."

electronics commanded the car's fuel-injection system, ignition, and vehicle diagnostics. By 1981, all Cadillacs could speak to service professionals through an expanded computer diagnostic system that could display up to 45 codes explaining an individual malfunction in the drive train.

Computer technology took more leaps and bounds in the 1980s and into the 1990s. Theft-deterrent systems, speed-sensitive steering and suspension, traction control, and even shifting would be dictated by a series of wires and computer chips, all working toward one goal—adding to the Cadillac driving experience.

Old favorites, such as leather-wrapped steering wheels, exotic wood trims, and rich leather seats, continued to enhance the Cadillac interiors, but there were also new favorites awaiting drivers by the late 1990s. Grasping advances in communication technology and using them to serve its drivers, Cadillac introduced OnStar in 1997. The service added immeasurable amounts of safety and convenience by offering directions, roadside emergency help, and door unlocking service. In the event a Cadillac's airbag is deployed, an OnStar advisor contacts the driver and can dispatch emergency personnel.

From Caterra's interior "techno finishes and jewel-like accents" to the SRX sport sedan's DVD navigation system and the Escalade's DVD entertainment system, Cadillac has luxury covered now and for many years into the future.

Bibliography

80 Years of Cadillac LaSalle. Walter M.P. McCall. Crestline Publishing Co., Sarasota, Florida (1982).

Barris Kustoms of the 1950s. George Barris and David Fetherston. Motorbooks International Publishers and Wholesalers, Osceola, Wisconsin (1994).

The Birth of Hot Rodding: The Story of the Dry Lakes Era. Robert Genat and Don Cox. MBI Publishing Company, St. Paul, Minnesota (2003).

The Cadillac LaSalle Self-Starter Annual, volume XXI. "The 1952 Cadillac Executive Special Two Passenger Speedster." Don Sherman. Cadillac La Salle Club Inc., Brentwood, California (1995).

Cadillac, The Standard of the World: The Complete History. Maurice D. Hendry. Automobile Quarterly Publications, Kutztown, Pennsylvania (1983).

Carrera Panamericana: The History of the Mexican Road Race, 1950-1954. Daryl E. Murphy. Motorbooks International Publishers and Wholesalers, Osceola, Wisconsin (1993).

The Cars of Lincoln-Mercury. George H. Dammann and James K. Wagner. Crestline Publishing Co., Sarasota, Florida (1987).

A Century of Style: 100 Years of American Car Design. Michael Lamm and Dave Holls. Lamm-Morada Publishing Company Inc. Stockton, California (1997).

Cunningham: The Life and Cars of Briggs Swift Cunningham. Dean Batchelor. Motorbooks International Publishers and Wholesalers, Osceola, Wisconsin (1993).

Standard Catalog of Cadillac, 1903-2000. Edited by James T. Lenzke. Krause Publications, Iola, Wisconsin (2000).